hindsight

hindsight

Untold Stories from 2020

Edited by Steve Fowler

First paperback edition March 2023

Cover design by Steve Leard

Hindsight logo by Hayley Higgs Design

ISBN (paperback) 9798375040424
ISBN (hardcover) 9798376729632

www.hindsightbook2020.com

For Uncle Michael

Contents

Part III: Summer

Part IV: Fall

Hindsight:
Untold Stories from 2020

Preface

"We're cutting Best Burgers," Kate said.

I leaned back in my chair and stared at the video call on my laptop screen. Just like that, our cover story was gone. Months of public polls, email outreach, spreadsheets, and burger tastings evaporated with four words. I couldn't believe it. Sure, none of our readers would know that our little regional lifestyle magazine had lost out on a great story – but I would. As the Food & Drink editor of that magazine, this had been my pet project.

"We're going to have to revisit the issue," Kate added.

I glanced at the calendar on my desk. Nine days to deadline. "How much of the issue?"

"All of it."

As expletives swirled around my mind, the ghost of a conversation from two weeks earlier came back to haunt me. We were still at the office, discussing the recent warning that schools and businesses may need to close to thwart the spread of a mysterious disease.

"Isn't this all a bit of an overreaction?" I said. "I mean they've been talking about this thing on NPR for two months now, and it seems the same as Ebola, Zika virus — any of those other outbreaks."

Kate drew a sharp breath and shook her head. "No…no, I think it's bad."

"I don't know," I shrugged. "It feels a bit melodramatic."

We developed a loose game plan for how to revise the issue and ended our video call. I turned on Governor Cuomo's press briefing to see how cases were trending while I reached out to contacts for stories.

Things didn't feel so "melodramatic" anymore. They felt frightening. Alien. Apocalyptic. Reports were emerging of sick patients lining hospital hallways and refrigerated tractor trailers serving as makeshift morgues. On screen, Cuomo emphasized the alarming shortage of ventilators in New York City. Even worse was the shocking news that had arrived the previous day: my uncle, my mom's brother, was in the hospital battling the very disease that had stopped the planet.

"He'd been feeling sick for a few days with cold and flu symptoms," my mother said when she called. "I guess the cold wouldn't go away on its own, and then he felt like he couldn't breathe. I think he got scared, so your aunt took him to the hospital."

"Jesus. That's not good."

"I know. And they wouldn't let anyone go in with him. I just feel so bad — he's there all alone."

That call commenced a nine-month barrage of bad news in which personal and public affairs grew entangled in a single mess of depression, anxiety, and confusion: A thousand people were dying from COVID every day. One of them was an elderly family friend living in a nursing home. Another close friend was let go from her job and had to file for unemployment; I offered sympathies, only to find out two weeks later that I was being furloughed and had to do the same thing. In the meantime, my uncle's lungs were filling with fluid, and the hospital staff was struggling to drain them. Images of scorched mountains and ashen koalas emerged from the wildfires in Australia, and my sister began to experience strange episodes where it felt like her throat was closing and she couldn't breathe and — wait, Trump said *what?* — then all of America watched a nine-minute video of a man being murdered by a police officer and soon there were protests across the country, but some people started to claim that murder wasn't murder and that death was deserved and not long after that I heard the word "plandemic" for the first time, and suddenly people were punching flight attendants and screaming at supermarket employees for being asked to wear a mask, which didn't seem like such a big deal, especially since my uncle, the one in the hospital with COVID, had died.

We met for his burial on a bright day in April. A handful of family members parked outside the iron gates of the cemetery, waiting for my aunt and her son to arrive. No one got out to say hello.

My aunt and cousin finally pulled in and led the rest of us around the hairpin curves of the cemetery. It seemed like there were more graves than usual. Finally, I spotted a couple of guys waiting by a casket laid over an open grave. Only my aunt and cousin were able to say goodbye. The rest of us waited on the pavement in makeshift masks, distant and silent, the only sound my aunt sobbing over my uncle's coffin. Her son held her weeping body up, but said nothing. In a month, he would graduate from college. There was not much chance of a commencement ceremony happening, given the circumstances; but there was one person he could no longer celebrate with.

And yet at the same time, my fiancée and I were among the lucky ones. No one in our nuclear families contracted COVID. We kept our jobs. We worked from home and never had to face the prospect of workplace biohazards; we cherished the fact that we never had to be apart and the extra time together made our relationship stronger.

Still, every day felt more like an impression of life rather than the real thing. Nowhere to go, nothing to do. Just restaurant take-out, jigsaw puzzles, walks around town. We binge watched television shows, but after a week, struggled to recall even basic plots and characters.

Visits with family had to be carefully coordinated, since both sets of parents fell into the high-risk category, which meant COVID-19 could prove especially fatal should they contract it. Before we had any type of extended visit, we quarantined ourselves for 14 days, no contact with anyone else except for grocery pickups. But at long last, we would arrive safe inside our family's exposure "bubble," and spend a week or so with the people we loved.

It was on one of these visits that the idea for this book came to me. A late summer afternoon, cicadas buzzing in the trees as I sat on the back deck. And it dawned on me: How often does everyone on the planet experience the same thing? How often is there any phenomenon that transcends geographical, cultural, political, and social boundaries? Birth, aging, and death are perhaps the only true unifiers. But for a time in 2020, everyone on Earth faced the same threat, the same dilemma, the same fear.

I immediately started working on a way to bottle this moment in time. I knew things would look different in hindsight – memory, like erosion, has a knack for smoothing things over – so it was imperative to start collecting stories as soon as possible. And while the pandemic was the unifying concept behind the book, what truly made 2020 distinct to me was that onslaught of mayhem, that avalanche of uncertainty that buried nearly everyone: COVID, wildfires, school closures, police violence, protests, bombs, elections, Supreme Court vacancies, election deniers, on and on and on.

In the end, we received stories from people in more than 28 countries. Not all of them could be included in this anthology, but all of them contained some flicker of humanity that I am better for reading. What I set out to do was to put together a history book – a record of important events told from the perspective of the average person. What I ended up with was a human book – a collection of critical days in people's lives during a time unlike any other in the last century.

In the pages that follow you'll find stories as unique as the people that wrote them: a Czech nurse who struggles against the pandemic fear and frenzy in New York City; an Australian woman who watches as her favorite hiking preserve is eaten by wildfires; a Texas man who wonders what will happen to his boomtown after the price of oil turns negative; a British father who works to help his mentally-ill son after yet another lockdown; an Alabama woman who is selected for one of the first COVID-19 vaccine trials; and many more.

Hindsight didn't turn out to be what I had originally envisioned, but then again, so little in life does.

After all, who envisions a pandemic?

— Steve Fowler

Prologue

Dyz Kovyt

Lenka Varekova
50, New York, United States

My family and I are separated by the ocean.

In the time of the pandemic, the ocean filled with worries, its waters deepened. Then it became still, with no ship to take me home now, or maybe ever.

"Leno, do you have *Dyz Kovyt* over there, too?" My father calls to check on me.

"Yes, Dad, but don't you worry, we have it under control. I need to go now; I can't be late for work." I put my scrubs on and walk into the morning darkness. My footsteps resonating through the empty streets of New York City, the city that never sleeps and never cries. Now still and quiet.

In the time of the pandemic, one becomes a liar.

I lied to my dad that I am ok.

I lied to my mom that I am protected.

I lied to both, that here in America, we are prepared to fight *Dyz Kovyt* – this COVID – because we all are in this together.

When all the protective supplies in the hospital were locked away to be distributed on an "as needed" basis, only to vanish moments later, I realized I am on my own. "As needed" is now, but the shelves are empty, the storage is locked, keys lost, managers on sick leave while assuring us we can handle the crisis:

We've got your back!

We received plenty of free stuff. Free coffee, free lunches, free goody bags with dry shampoo, snacks, instant soup, underwear – but no masks.

Distracted by the free stuff and body count, we did not notice when the nursing supervisors disappeared and the priests came with Bibles and plastic rosaries. When the psychologists and wellness specialists brought calming lavender, meditation apps, and CBD oils, I followed their instructions. I hung the lavender sachet around my neck, ready to smell it in case I felt overwhelmed or scared.

We got you ready. Now go do your jobs.

Are you sending me to fight an invisible enemy that could be deadly, giving me the orders to fight from your warm bedrooms? Where do I get my own protection, my own mask, my own shield? Where do I get my own courage?

Do I have to go? How dedicated am I to saving the lives of others? Would calling out sick tomorrow save my own life?

"Leno, did they give you a mask?"

"Of course, Dad. Don't worry, I got two."

Getting my first N95 felt like having a heroin dealer come to my house. On the first night of New York Fashion Week, the hideous N95 became the hottest item in town, and to get it, you needed to know somebody.

Luckily, I did.

My hair was getting wet from the spring mist when the car with the dark windows finally stopped in front of my house. The two men with bandana scarfs, dark circles under their eyes, unshaven and haggard, had driven all the way from uptown.

"Did you bring it?"

My nursing friends from the better-supplied hospital handed me the brown paper bag through the rolled-down window. I grabbed it and slipped it under my sweater.

"Is this really it?"

My heart was beating fast as I clutched the bag tight to my body.

"Good luck," they said, and drove away.

It felt like I just got my first pair of Louboutin shoes, took a first bite of a freshly baked croissant in Paris, and won an airplane ticket around the world all at the same time. I watched the car speeding away on the deserted street then ran upstairs to look at it. N95 sounded like a good deal: 95% chance to live, 5% chance to die. That is, if it fits you correctly. The ugly duck beak disfiguring my face, pulling my hair, and suffocating my breath came with the surprising comfort that now I have a chance to survive.

My second N95 was donated to me by a stranger who mailed it to my house with a touching note: "I hope that this mask keeps you protected for at least a little while. You are, and will be, remembered as a hero."

I treated them as gold, disinfecting and airing them in the brown paper bags in my home basement after each shift.

Having my two treasures made me feel braver. I took a deep breath, put my first N95 mask on, and walked on the COVID unit. There, we did the best we could.

There, I lied many times using the word "stable."

"Yes, he is stable!"

I used the word stable as a shield to separate the loud, direct question from the real, crushing answer. Stable, the word neutral enough to avoid talking about what both of us on the opposite sides of the phone receivers knew, connected by the telephone wire, connected by thin invisible hope.

I was grateful for the face shields ordered from the hardware stores and handmade by strangers from flimsy plastic and Velcro straps. Not because I trusted it to protect me from the virus, but because it fogged and hid my tears.

I did not know any of my coworkers, as we all met for the first time on the unit to which we were randomly deployed. Somebody thought of writing our names on the face shields to call each other for help when we needed to turn the heavy bodies face down to expand our patient's lungs. We all looked the same, geared up like hockey players for a game that had no winner, our eyes tired, reflecting fading smiles buried deep underneath the masks.

When passing the eighteen-wheeler mobile morgue truck parked outside the hospital, I thought of those I took care of yesterday in bright isolation rooms filled with beeping sounds. It terrified me that now they were here, their bodies waiting to be reunited with their loved ones, their names placed on the burial waiting list.

The engine hummed, maintaining the dark and cold.

From far away, my dad called again. "Leno, is *Dyz Kovyt* real? Our neighbor told us that it has something to do with the phone chips and we should eat more cabbage to protect ourselves."

"Dad, I do not think that this is true, but please be careful. And yes, eat as much cabbage as you like, the virus doesn't care. And please do not worry about me. I am fine."

I pretended I was fine during the day but kept waking up during the night in panic that I didn't have my mask on. In my dream I saw my mom calling for help, waving her arms at me trapped behind the ICU glass door. Our unit ran out of plastic gowns and without the protection I could not enter her isolation room. I walked by, pretending I did not see her.

In the time of pandemic, one becomes a thief.

Every day on the COVID unit, I stole the last moments of someone's life that did not belong to me. In those moments I became whomever my patients needed. I was the love of the tall, bearded man's life, I was the childhood friend who broke the thin woman's favorite blue crayon, I was the secret lover of the family man that nobody knew about, I was the runaway son of the proud businessman, I was the best friend of the Hasidic man who came to apologize for something long forgotten. I stole those last moments from the people who were supposed to be there with them instead of me. I stole the last moment from a nurse who could not be there with her brother because she was taking care of other dying patients in another hospital on the opposite side of the city.

I held my patients' hands in my own, protected by ill-fitting purple gloves.

Scent of lavender in the air.

"Leno, do you still have *Dyz Kovyt* over there?"

Part I: Winter

Resorting

Hannah Lund
30, Shanghai, China

As I floated in the resort's pool, I couldn't believe I'd actually pulled it off. I'd made it through heightened airport security in a virus outbreak, wearing an N95 respirator mask for an entire day. I'd even made it through customs while surrounded by travelers who seemed to be competing for who could snuffle, huff, and jostle around the most.

Take that, virus! I thought, splashing my feet in the cool water. *I beat you!*

I mentally took note that symptoms would appear, should they appear, in four to five days. I took a deep, investigative breath. All clear.

The other resort-goers seemed oblivious to our close call. Families with tanned skin and serene smiles ordered poolside smoothies one after the other, gaggles of girls in swimsuits ordering Corona beers while bobbing on inflatable pink flamingo floaties. They weren't escaping anything. People arrived at a resort intentionally, not washing up as if they'd jumped ship before the Titanic hit the iceberg.

My nerves still thrummed from my long trip from Shanghai. I was like Indiana Jones, had his treasure been a strawberry daiquiri. It already felt worth it, even though I'd never "resorted" before. Resorting always seemed extravagant. And by extravagant I mean expensive. Being a graduate student hadn't welcomed extravagant trips like this. But I'd graduated, and Katie, my friend who would be joining me at Turtle Bay Dive Resort, suggested we ought to resort, using the now-familiar cajoling phrase "Treat yo'self!" We could do everything we wanted in Moalboal without having to walk too far. Who could want anything more?

Another deep breath. Still clear.

Katie wasn't too concerned about the coronavirus, at least not so when I called her in a panic the day before. She knew there were outbreaks in China, but said we could avoid that. I pretended to not be that concerned about it, still lightheartedly saying to "Please" wear a mask on the plane and "Have hand sanitizer ha-ha!"

But Wuhan, where the virus was first detected, had just been put into lockdown to contain it. The virus was raging there, but not here.

Another deep breath.

From my perch, I looked up at deep blue skies and cotton ball clouds, the breeze lilting in the air. Turtle Bay was a collection of cream-colored villas ringing a pool, a restaurant, and a dive shop situated by the shore. Located on a quiet part of an island in the Philippines, it felt about as far away from the fear as we could get. A great place, if any, to hole up while a virus snuck around, unwanted and invisible elsewhere.

I closed my eyes, letting the languages I didn't understand drift around me. At last, I had an excuse to not know what was going on. I could finally be uninformed for a while and not feel too guilty about it.

Some of the guests around me sniffled from colds, wet coughs rattling out of them.

I breathed deeper. *Four to five days.*

That's when I heard Chinese.

It's no use pretending I didn't eavesdrop. Of course I did. I'd spent the better part of nine years learning the language. And now, I could listen in on gossip while the speakers dismissed my ability at the sight of my blonde hair.

The people speaking Chinese were a family of three, wrangling their beach gear and applying sunscreen. They spoke in clear, standard Mandarin about mundane things like setting up their towels, whether they would go snorkeling later, the like. After several moments of inner debate after I'd stepped out of the pool, I went over to greet them.

"Hi, where are you from?" I asked in English.

"China," the father said.

"Where in China?"

"Shanghai."

I immediately switched to Chinese. "Oh my god, I live in Shanghai, too! I work there!"

·

The man's face lit up and his wife came over to breeze through the usual questions: where I was from, what I was doing in Shanghai, what brought me to China in the first place.

"It's so amazing that all the way out here, we meet someone else from Shanghai!" the woman said.

"It's *yuanfen*," the man said, using the catchall term for luck, chance encounters, and anything that felt vaguely fortuitous.

"Right! And what a great time not to be in Shanghai, huh?" I said.

They faltered. I wondered if I should have alluded to the virus at all. They'd probably come to forget about it for a spell, too, to actually enjoy their Lunar New Year holiday. But there was no way they hadn't been thinking of it.

"Oh yes," the woman said with a solemn expression. "We were very careful coming over. Washed our hands, wore masks."

"Oh, me too," I said, almost defensively.

"We were very careful," the man agreed.

"Oh, I'm sure. I was, too."

"Shanghai should be okay, since the hospitals are good and public awareness is also pretty high," the woman said.

"Oh yes, Shanghai is quite safe," I said. There was an awkward silence. "I do feel sorry for the people of Wuhan, though," I added.

"Yes, they are very *xinku*," the woman said.

"Very, very *xinku*," I agreed.

"The doctors, too."

"*Xinku* doctors, indeed."

12

We were smiling magnanimously at each other. But I knew what was up. We'd gone through the motions of absolving ourselves through *xinku*. We were acknowledging how dangerous it was to travel in the middle of an outbreak, which meant we were aware, therefore in the clear. With *xinku*, we were showing sympathy and expressing dismay at Wuhan's difficulties. But *xinku* goes deeper than that; it is the phrase you use when someone is making a sacrifice you recognize to be difficult, but you are not willing to make yourself. It is the American equivalent of "Appreciate it!" – you recognize the hassle but are glad the other person is taking care of it.

We rattled off statistics about the virus to each other. ("Did you know the virus could survive on surfaces? We wash our hands." "Did you know they're sending in doctors from other provinces to help Wuhan? How brave." "Companies suspended travel to and from Hubei. We're so lucky.") My heart raced the more we talked. Did they get it? Did they understand that I'd done my best, but was still a little selfish? Could we forgive each other for not sacrificing our vacations for something we didn't understand?

Eventually we smiled and said we would exchange WeChats and probably see each other around the resort at some point. We parted ways.

Days later, I'd already forgotten about the exchange, having become an expert at resorting. You just had to let yourself forget. Or at least hit pause on the world outside the walls. And you drank smoothies. Daily. The world outside just blurred.

That is, until it didn't.

A few days in, I woke up one morning with a stuffed nose.

I felt my forehead. No fever. No cough. I took a deep, investigative breath. All clear. "It's just a cold," I said, after I told Katie I couldn't scuba dive like this. "Initial symptoms of the virus are sore throat and fever. I don't have a fever." After several moments, I added: "Just, you know, wash your hands."

I imagined the smug look on the virus's face for my panic. "Take that, human!" it would likely cackle, in what I assumed would be a rattled voice. "This time, I beat you!"

I decided to take a nap for the rest of the morning, some corner of my mind thinking my body could be like a computer, that if you just turned it on and off again, the problems would go away.

In my half-dream, half-wake state, I saw an old hag before me, pointing to the scar on the bridge of my nose from the N95 mask I'd worn throughout my daylong trip from Shanghai.

"That's a wart, dearie," she said. "I know what you are."

But she didn't have to tell me. I was *xinku*. Wuhan was *xinku*. The world was drowning in *xinku*.

Jiayou

Tanya Angell Allen
49, Connecticut, United States

My husband and eight-year-old son and I drank hot chocolate and stamped our feet in the February cold as we waited for New Haven's 2020 Dragon and Lion Dance Parade. Carlos and his four-year-old joined us. They'd wanted to see the Lunar Parade in New York's Chinatown, but Carlos had decided not to travel due to fear of a mysterious virus in China. Other U.S. cities had also canceled their Chinese New Year celebrations because of the virus, but it was on the other side of the planet. It all seemed a little dramatic.

I hoped to see the parade in New York sometime myself, but since we lived in Guilford, Connecticut, and it was cold, it was easier to get to the New Haven one. I was trying to celebrate as many holidays as I could, hoping to subdue my depression over the way politicians were using hate to divide the country. I liked observing holidays from other cultures and using them to peek at parts of the world. In studying holidays I'd learned that there are no "global" ones celebrated by every country on Earth. There have also been few global events that have affected all of us. Even the World Wars didn't touch all of our countries. Perhaps the main thing that everyone in the world has witnessed, albeit within a few hours of each other depending on where they are situated on earth, is the waxing and waning of the moon.

The Chinese New Year itself begins on the first day of the first new moon of each year. The celebrations end when the moon is full. The 2020 parade in New Haven was tiny. There were a few red, blue, and gold dragons made out of cardboard and fabric carried by lines of schoolchildren and other New Haven community members. The Yale China Association and the Yale Police departments walked by with banners emblazoned with their organization's names. The Federal Credit Union passed out tiny hand sanitizer bottles attached to keychains. The highlight was the appearance of two Chinese lions from the Wan Chi Ming Hung Gar Institute of New York City. They were accompanied by a small band of men in red and gold who played cymbals and drums. One lion was white, the other yellow. Each had two people inside making their paws walk and their ears twitch and their mouths open and close. They padded slowly up the street, weaving over to the sidewalks when people held out red envelopes. Bystanders put coins or bills into the envelopes and placed them in the lion's mouths so that they could be pulled out by hands within. The envelopes were decorated with pictures of rats, as 2020 was the Year of the Rat.

The lions danced for a while at the Asian Food store, blessing it. We did a clumsy dance on the sidewalk at the same time, trying to keep warm. "It's ok," I murmured to my son as he complained about how freezing it was. Finally, people and lions grouped at the end of the street. Mayor Justin Elicker gave a speech, first in Mandarin and then in English. He spoke of Changsha, which is New Haven's sister city, and of Wuhan, where the mysterious virus was centered. We were shown signs with Chinese characters on them: 加 油 . We were taught how to say the characters: "*Jiayou*," which sounds like "gee-ah-yo."

In a way similar to how the English word "cool" can mean "cold" but can also mean "great," *jiayou* has multiple meanings. It is often used at sports events to mean "Go team, go!" or "You can do it!" In our case, the word meant "Stay strong."

"*Jiayou*!"

The Yale China Association had our crowd shout the word out while they filmed us. They said they would send the clips to the people of China.

Wuhan was under lockdown, but apartment dwellers there had been videotaped shouting to each other through their windows: "Wuhan *jiayou*!"

"*Jiayou*!" We shouted in New Haven. "*Jiayou*!"

I felt bad for the people in Wuhan, but I didn't put as much heart into the exclamations as I could have. I was worrying about how to get my son comfortable and how to find my friends and wondering when the speeches would end.

When the lions began dancing, my child was so cold that he screamed in pain, but the drums and the cymbals were so loud that no one noticed. One lion rose above us on stilts. Someone fed him a head of lettuce with a stick. After a few minutes the lion spat leaves of lettuce out so that they rained on the crowd like money.

People on the street and in the diner next to us looked on, heads tilted, mouths open. Next year before the Lunar Festival, I thought, looking at the people warm inside the diner, we'll meet our friends there instead of on the street.

We left before the end of the dance. Carlos and his son left before us due to the cold. I saw my friend Jeannette briefly on the sidewalk in her bright red coat. I reached out and hugged her. Nilakshi and her family were somewhere across the street. Maila and her family were somewhere there, too. We texted together frantically, but my child was too upset for us to meet up with them. "We're going to head out," I texted with frigid fingers. "I'll see you next week."

During the night after the festival, I woke up around one in the morning. I stumbled downstairs to feed our own small lion-cats in the kitchen. I looked out the window and thought that it had snowed. The ground was so bright that trees cast shadows on our lawn. The full moon glowed like an icicle's rounded end.

I thought of the citizens of Wuhan. This time I did feel the sympathy that I had struggled to conjure during the Festival.

"*Jiayou*," I whispered, thinking of the people of China looking up at the sky.

Postpartum

Blair Hurley
34, Ontario, Canada

She was born in the first week of March, and by her first doctor's appointment at two days old, the world had changed. Our doctor had been out of Canada on vacation and had to self-isolate for two weeks, so we were forced to take her to a walk-in clinic for her first real check-up. By then, COVID-19 was spreading, or had been spreading for months, and we hadn't understood the danger. We sat tensely in the crowded waiting room with our newborn, fastened to her car seat between us, wondering what illnesses the people around us had. A child coughed beside us and we looked away, as though by pretending it hadn't happened, we could somehow keep ourselves safe.

My husband and I are Americans new to Canada, still learning to navigate the health care system, still pleasantly surprised when we discover another expansive benefit offered to Canadians without charge. I was on the edge of a titanic life shift, alone with my husband in a foreign country, and parenthood was another foreign place, its shores unknown. In the weeks before her birth, there was no talk of coronavirus, besides news from China that seemed very far away. I re-organized the toys and wipes and minute little onesies in drawers, nervous as a horse before a storm.

When we arrived late at night at the labor floor of the hospital, the halls were dim and peaceful, the nurses calm and attentive. She came quickly, just a few hours after I stumbled through the hospital doors, the epidural merciful and immediate. Somehow the fact of having a baby – becoming a mother – did not become fully real until the moment she was placed on my chest: this crying, squirming, tomato-red little creature who suddenly needed me in awesome ways. I felt my life change, felt the surprise of it. Then her need, instant and demanding, took over, and I fumbled to hold her, to feed her, to fulfill those many needs. The duty to do so, both an immediate burden and a joy in a way I did not expect. When they briefly swept her out of my arms to check her breathing, I felt the immediate loss, a kind of longing absence that minutes before I had not known.

We didn't hear much about the virus for the two days I spent in the hospital, fragile and bleeding, my husband curled on the couch, her in a plexiglass bassinet beside us, fascinating and beautiful. The outside world was the view from my window and nothing more – parking lot, roll of muddy hills, watery spring sunrise. The world could wait. We returned home and consumed ourselves with learning how to feed her, diaper her, soothe her, overwhelmed and exhausted. My sister came to help and slipped into the country days before the borders closed. My mother had died five years ago. I knew I'd miss her when I was holding my daughter in my arms, but now her absence was sharp and frightening. No one in our locked-down household knew what we were doing. We didn't know what it meant when she sighed or moaned or cried, we didn't know how to hold her or feed her. I remembered the breathless feeling I had when I first took the test and saw the faint blue line and felt suddenly responsible for a life. She needed me, and the world was falling apart.

We returned to the hospital a few days later to visit the breastfeeding clinic, and a hospital employee questioned us at the door about our travel history. We sat behind discreet curtained spaces, listening to the coos and gentle murmurs of other mothers struggling with latching and letdown. But the threat was growing each day. The next time we came to the hospital, two nurses with surgical masks asked us to stop behind a red line while we answered questions about our recent travel history and whether we were showing symptoms. "Don't touch anything," the nurses told us, their faces blank and inscrutable behind their masks.

A nurse gingerly handed us a referral form, touching the paper with just the tips of her fingers, and I did the same holding the other end. We sanitized our hands whenever we entered a room, tried to remember exactly everything we touched. The lactation clinic was empty and dark this time, with just one appointment at a time to minimize exposure. We sat in the ominous quiet and I spoke to my daughter, encouraging her to nurse. She looked so small in my arms. We tried not to touch our faces.

A birth can seem like a cataclysm for the body, and for the mind as well; health care workers kept asking me if I was experiencing symptoms of postpartum depression, and assured me that even if I didn't now, I might very well months down the line. Recovery is not just a question of healing; it's also a radical shifting of what you imagine for your life, and what the world now holds. My body is a postpartum body, and my world is now a postpartum world. We're living in a time that feels apocalyptic, both personally and on a global scale. In the night, I find myself rising when I should be taking my meager sleep, watching my daughter's chest rise and fall, both reassured and frightened as I see it continue to do so.

At our next hospital appointment, two nurses in masks, gowns, and face shields asked questions from a ten-foot distance. Visitors were not allowed. The hospital was eerily silent and empty. In other hospitals in Toronto, in New York, we knew beds were lined up in the hallways; somewhere in carefully cordoned off wings of this building, people were ill and dying. A doctor moving past us in a mask and disposable gown saw our girl in her carrier and said wearily, "I wish I were that young."

We holed up with cases of formula and diapers, as the injunction to shelter in place became cemented. I scrolled through the news with one hand while she slept on my chest, feeling overwhelming relief that she arrived on time and not later, as many firstborns do. Tried to enjoy our newborn in a haze of sleep deprivation and worry. Tried to learn how to soothe her, feed her, rotate her in the bassinet so her soft moldable skull would form the right shape. Tummy time while Trudeau and Trump gave speeches on the television. Changed our clothes when we went out for groceries and wiped down the boxes and wondered what invisible dangers we were carrying with us. I heard from my friends that for them, and the millions of others sheltering in place around the world, that their days passed in a haze, alternating between dreamlike drifting through the day and heart-thudding insomnia. There might be no closer experience to this than the early days of having a baby. Among fear and worry and uncertainty, there are bursts of beauty. The minutes are long; the weeks are short.

In emails and Zoom meetups, I heard from fellow mothers and soon-to-be-mothers. My pregnant friends were terrified. They were facing the prospect of not having spouses or doulas in delivery rooms. Meeting their OBGYNs only by teleconference. Learning to take their own blood pressure and self-monitor for signs of pre-eclampsia. These women wondered if they'd be laboring in surgical masks, struggling to breathe clearly, or if they contracted the virus, getting separated from their newborns. I remembered the instant sense of loss I felt when she was first taken from my arms. My friends wondered how their careful birth plans would be shredded to nothing.

Mothers judge themselves more harshly than anyone else for their shortcomings. My friends spoke of stopping breastfeeding as the first failure, the sign that perfect motherhood would always be out of reach. We were in unprecedented times. Parenthood, too, is the experience in life for which there is no precedent.

I feel like crying one day when I realize no one but my husband and my sister have held her for the first three months of her life. No one has cuddled her and oohed and aahed over her accomplishments except through a screen. But maybe it's just the hormones leveling off; I can't trust my own body and its emotional responses these days. I'm struggling to read its new signals of tiredness and hunger and pain the same way I struggle to read hers. She is a new landscape, as is my own body. It's stretched in places, strangely tight in others. I was never able to have a follow-up appointment with my OBGYN, and so I don't know if I am okay, or what being okay postpartum really means.

I am lucky to have a good sleeper. Three months old and she is sleeping seven hours through the night, quiet and dreamy, her

Steve Fowler

long dark lashes beautiful against her smooth cheek. I should be taking advantage of this, finally recouping my own sleep, but I am not. Instead, I am waking every two or three hours, dimly aware of myself, of something wrong – am I alone somehow when I shouldn't be? No, my husband is sleeping beside me. The baby is beside me in her bassinet. But she is not inside me anymore, not a part of me, and my body feels this to be wrong. I keep waking with dreams that the baby is missing. I dream that the baby has been kidnapped and we have to scrounge together the ransom money. "Where is the baby?" I wake in a panic, demanding of my husband.

She is there, sleeping beside me, but the process of separation has already begun, she is not a part of me anymore and so my body aches its loss.

When she's three months old, when she's six months, ten months old, we begin to realize, this will not be over any time soon; this is the altered landscape of her first year of life, and it's our job to make the best of things, to be present for her, not dreaming of other things we might have been doing. Here it is, her babyhood, and there won't be another chance to witness it, so we'd better show up, again and again and again, the way parents must do. There are consolations. Her nose-crinkling smile seems to make the world crack and slip gooily away from me like the yolk of an egg. I'm there living in her bright eyes and for a moment we're one thing again.

Feeling that haze of postpartum emotion: joy and wonder and sadness that my mother cannot be here with me now to tell me what to do, or to delight in her granddaughter's little nose, her grasping fingers, her funny faces. Feeling regret that my

24

father back in the U.S. will not be able to see his first grandchild in person for months; this first strange year of her life will belong only to my husband and me, quarantined from the world of people who love her already and wish they could meet her. I spend the sleepy days worrying for my pregnant friends. Trying to remember that we'd be living this hermited life anyway.

The mothers told me that these difficult times would pass: the newborn phase, because of the sleep deprivation, is only a dim memory in their own experiences of parenthood. Parents have to have faith in the passage of time. Everything, the mothers told me, is a phase. Both the terrible times and the good ones will pass, and next week you'll be wondering where they went, with relief or sadness.

When these long nights and blurry months pass, I believe the exhaustion of pumping breastmilk, nursing, rising in the dark will begin to ease just the slightest bit. I believe by that time we'll emerge into the world just as millions of others will, blinking in the sunlight. I don't know what kind of world we'll be carrying her into, whether it will be unrecognizably altered from the one I knew, but that is the thing parents never know, and gamble on anyway, that there will be a world to come into. There are the people who help keep it going: the nurses and doctors who cared for me and my girl with such solemn, tender dedication. There are the people who risk everything, determined to make it better: the protesters fighting for justice. I'll have so much to explain to her. She hasn't seen any of it yet. I'll have to tell her, "This is the world."

Apocalypse

Nellie Warren
17, Dublin, Ireland

It happened sometime during English class. I was in my fifth year – that's the penultimate year in Irish secondary school – so we were covering some poet, maybe Bishop or Boland. At the beginning of the class, our teacher told us, "There's supposed to be an announcement soon."

None of us had any doubt as to what it would be. Lockdown had been imminent, especially since our neighboring countries were taking the leap, clearing out the streets and shutting down schools and workplaces, forcing the world inside their homes for a fortnight. A few days prior, we had an assembly which warned us to socially distance from each other, an ironic announcement since the assembly was held in a room where the chairs were so close together that we all nearly sat on top of each other. And after that assembly there were no real enforcements made by the school. Not until Thursday.

When the bell rang for the next class, the eight of us who took art ran down to reunite with our clay pieces, imagining that we'd have today and tomorrow to finish them, and that by Saturday we'd be locked down.

We swung into the classroom, all hurrying to make the most of our hour-long class. My art teacher glanced up from her laptop. She was a calm person with a mellow voice, but there was something like an alarm bell ringing from her throat. "Did you hear?" she asked.

We hadn't, but we could guess. "Are we off for a few weeks, starting Monday?" my friend blurted.

"No," corrected the teacher, "starting now."

Confusion erupted. I think I asked if she was sure a few times until I read the information myself. Non-essential businesses will shut down, schools will go online, everybody should remain inside. For two weeks, starting now.

Apparently, the staff was going to have an emergency meeting during lunch in about fifty minutes. In the meantime, our teacher advised us to leave soaking wet towels over our clay sculptures, so that hopefully they'd be preserved, and we could finish them after the two weeks. We rushed to and from the sink with drenched towels, the water dripping on the floor and pooling at each sculpture's base.

At lunch everybody flocked to the hall. The stage was set up at the front of the room – it was *Seachtain na Gaeilge*, an annual festival celebrating Irish culture and language. The following day our Irish teacher was planning to hold a concert to celebrate, as was school tradition. I was going to host. The Irish teacher gathered the group with a flat smile.

"Well, folks," she said. And didn't elaborate. She didn't need to. We all felt the odd new weight – not heavy like a brick, but rather like a bird on your shoulder. It has feathers and wings, but claws that dig deep through the skin.

We carried our birds on our shoulders to the stage, where most students ate in relative silence, save for the murmurs. When the teachers emerged from their meeting, we were told we'd be going home – and we'd need to take the contents of our lockers with us.

Many of us tried to protest – we had so many books and copies and notes, and some of us lived an hour away or more. Couldn't we just leave them here until the two weeks were up? But no, they needed to do an intensive clean of the entire school, lockers included. We weren't to leave a trace of ourselves. We had to take everything. As I called my dad and looked around the school for my sister among the fourth years, I saw that teachers were handing out garbage bags to put books in.

I found my sister, who said our dad had texted and was on his way. I started emptying the contents of my locker into the black plastic bag: the heavy history books and the biology notes I doodled on, the empty water bottle I thought I'd lost, broken earphones. I became suddenly aware of the bodies moving around me. The grunting, breathing, grabbing hands – so many boys don't wash their hands. The year before, some girls in my class had done a swab of all the door handles in school for a science project. The boy's bathroom door was the worst. They found a UTI on the girl's bathroom door, too – I don't even know how you find that on a door handle. But no door handle in the school was without something disgusting. I saw it myself in the biology lab. The dishes were labeled: maths room, geography room, history, English, Irish, classics, French, business, staff room, on and on. There was fur on the gelatin in some cases; I didn't know what that meant and didn't want to ask. Bacteria decorating a petri dish, blooming in white and yellow dots, like ugly little fairy lights.

This disease was more than germs though, wasn't it? It was killing people.

I had already known the world was ending. I wasn't stupid, I knew the planet was dying in countless ways. But right then it felt like the apocalypse had begun from our school hall. Teenagers swarming around, shouting into phones and at each other. Black garbage bags burst with the weight of books or flapped in the air like anarchist flags. When I returned to the art room to grab my portfolio, a second year lay on the floor with his books spilling out of a bag. I ran past him, and behind me heard another second-year girl asking anxiously if he was okay.

"Okay? Am I okay? Yeah, I'm brilliant. I feel wonderful. Fucking thanks for asking."

On my way back up the stairs, he was still on the floor, apologizing to the girl.

While we waited for our parents to come get us, we left our trash bags in the hall, slouched against each other like lumpy, plastic monsters, and went to whatever class we were supposed to be having. On the way up to the French classroom, I drummed along the wall with my knuckles to calm myself down, and let my teeth knock together in my mouth. I looked down at my school uniform, and wondered if it'd be the last time I'd wear it. In the final year of secondary, our school allowed students to wear their own clothes. What if I never came back to the building for the remainder of fifth year?

I quickly dismissed the thought with a smile. Even if we'd be gone longer than two weeks, we'd be back before the end of the school year. It was only March, anyway.

In the French room, our teacher told us COVID conspiracies. It reminded me of being in second year the day after Trump won the U.S. presidential election, and we spent our French class listening to our teacher dole out conspiracies, though he refused to refer to them as such. I brought it up again, and we laughed; a moment of levity amidst the madness. I lay my head on the desk, teeth chattering.

Not long afterwards, I dragged my garbage bag to my dad's car in the nearby parking lot. As I threw my bag into the back seat, I realized I had forgotten my umbrella, and ran back inside for it.

Somewhere in the corner of me, I was looking forward to the two weeks off. I was – and am – an anxious introvert, and even though I loved my friends and didn't hate school like I used to, every social interaction shut my eyelids a little further, and by the end of the school day I'd be groggy on the bus, and then silently watching YouTube videos or reading at home, leaving my homework to the last minute. By the weekend I'd sleep in until two or three in the afternoon.

Staying at home would mean nobody but my family physically seeing me. No echoey school halls or first years being fire hazards in the corridors. No tense or nerve-wracking teacher or student interactions. No Dublin bus – thank god for that. I could work on my writing and art projects, paint more, read more, watch more movies. For two whole weeks, I could recharge.

It seemed that most people were at least looking forward to two weeks "off" school – not counting the online classes. When I ran back inside to grab my umbrella, the hall was mostly cleared of students, save for a friend, who sat at a table, blinking at her phone.

We talked briefly as I picked my umbrella up from behind the chairs stacked up at the back of the room, complaining about the lockers, laughing about the situation. Just as I left the hall again, I called to her, "See you in two weeks!"

"Two weeks!" she repeated, grinning with a raised hand, a number of bracelets spiraling down her wrist.

The Unique Moral Distress of COVID-19 Deaths

Joyeeta G. Dastidar
41, New York, United States

During the first peak, infected patients were sequestered away in the high towers of the hospital, isolated and removed from family. No visitors were allowed, and not just because of fear of spreading the virus, but also because there wasn't enough personal protective equipment for hospital staff, not to mention family. There were means to bridge the gap a bit: doctors, physician assistants, nurses, palliative care practitioners, and pastoral services used tablets and cell phones so family members could at least connect digitally.

In many cases, arranging for families to see their loved ones seemed like the most essential service one could provide for an illness with no proven effective treatments to date back then. We did this knowing it wasn't the same as the soothing presence of a family member continuously at bedside stroking their loved one's hand. While we believed in the need to minimize visitors to contain the spread of the virus, there was a disconnect between the science and epidemiology behind that knowledge versus the awareness of the high emotional price the patient and family paid by not being together at the most vulnerable time in their lives. It felt as though the healthcare system was inflicting further harm to already distressed patients and families.

I remember one elderly woman was terrified to be alone, fearful that death was upon her.

"I'm dying!" she shouted. "I'm dying!" The panic palpable in her voice and touch as she frantically grasped at me. I stood there paralyzed, knowing I should stay longer, while simultaneously thinking of the long list of patients still waiting to be tended to.

As COVID cases climbed, ICU resources and ventilators grew increasingly scarce. At my institution, where I'd been for almost a decade, my workplace became unrecognizable: mini-ICUs were created on each floor, ICU patients were roomed together, operating rooms and post-anesthesia care units were converted to create even more ICU beds, and staff from across the country came to help out. Hospitals created ventilator triage allocation guidelines to help doctors decide which patients were placed on ventilators when the inevitable shortage hit. But the question became, "Who decides who lives or dies?" and "What if they were wrong?" After all, COVID was uncharted territory for everyone.

Every evening, at 7 p.m., the city would honor healthcare workers by making some noise, with whatever instruments they had nearby ranging from clanging on pots and pans to blowing an air horn. This, I appreciated. On a day off, there wasn't much to do other than go for a walk along the streets of New York City. I wandered up to Times Square, where the usual advertisements on the jumbo screens were taken over by a "Not all superheroes wear capes" campaign. The superhero label was no doubt created with good intentions, but the involuntary nature of the heroism was uncomfortable. While grateful to be able to help out, I also wondered if there were limits to what would be expected of us.

In a different hospital room, another patient was awaiting intubation (having a breathing tube put in) in order to be placed on a ventilator. She asked me if she would die. My instinct was to tell her no. It was the only kind answer. But there were so many patients who passed away before her, I didn't actually *know* if she'd pull through, and I didn't want to lie to her either. I paused for a fraction of a second before I answered her. She instantly picked up on my moment of hesitation in responding to her question. In her mind, this slight break before responding seemed akin to a death pronouncement.

I tried to backpedal, listing factors that supported her survival, pointing out her relative youth and health, but I was trying to convince myself as much as I was trying to convince her. I stood by her bedside patting her arm and murmuring reassurances, not knowing what else to do. When I left her room, I felt guilty as I thought of the grave disservice I'd done, fomenting panic in a patient at a time when calm was needed.

Going through the motions day after day, I'd fallen into a bit of a routine. As the numbers peaked, healthcare workers who had been labeled heroes became victims caught in the fray, an increasing number of us succumbing to the illness itself. My hospital belonged to a conglomerate of hospitals in the area. They began posting an online bulletin of employees who had passed from COVID-19 consisting of a photo, the employee's name, position, and hospital. The visual death toll was COVID-19's version of roll call. Most faces I didn't recognize; the organization I worked for was enormous, and they were from other hospitals or departments I didn't interact with. I did notice that most of the medical workers' faces were brown or black, just as those of the patients I had been pronouncing (confirming to be dead). Then, one day, I saw the face of a social worker I knew smiling back at me. I wondered how it happened, did they catch it at work, how their family took it.

They were so friendly, so lively the last time I saw them. We had discussed the discharge plan for a patient before COVID. Now, they were no more, one soul among the many our city was losing in droves.

Sanitize

Gabe Porter
23, Ohio, United States

I delicately open the bottle of hand sanitizer so as to reapply another sickly sticky coat onto my fingers. A mucus forms around my hands as I do this over the course of my workday. The alcohol contained within the gel burns miniscule cuts and scrapes never seen. My fingerprints feel irrevocably changed by the overzealous accumulation of the all-cleaning syrup. I try and wipe the excess off onto my clothes. Despite this, there still exists deep under my fingernails the remnants of the viscous liquid. I stop what I am doing and stare at it. The glistening globs look like teardrops from an alien. I start to lose focus as fog fills my glasses. I move my mouth – open shut open shut – as to readjust the mask, hoping to reach a miracle placement that allows for clear eyesight. I get to a place that alleviates some of the buildup before I give up and move my glasses with my tacky hands. I do this fast enough to see a customer approach me without a mask. Their face turns into a dagger pointed towards my heart. I hide the anxiety by subtly backing away, my feet barely leaving the floor. Anything to just put distance between me and the invisible particles spewed from the weapon of their face. They ask a question, I mutter a response.

I don't breathe until they have left. Long inhale, long exhale. I allow myself to dissociate, just ever so slightly. I start to go back to work, breaking open boxes to stack all the products. Before I do, however, I reach into my pocket and pull out the tiny, almost empty vile. I delicately open the bottle of sanitizer so as to reapply another sickly sticky coat onto my fingers.

Part II: Spring

As I Slept

Julie Aitcheson

47, West Virginia, United States

The start of the pandemic found me at my parents' home in West Virginia after my latest stint as an international educator. My world had gone from the size of the Tanzanian savannah to small town U.S.A. in the blink of a red-eye flight, and that was fine. That was my rhythm. Then, COVID-19 sparked in the U.S. and began jumping from person to person like a cinder between haystacks until the whole country was on fire. When a "stay at home" order was issued in West Virginia on March 24, the Appalachian trailhead parking lots nearby started to look like Walmart on a Saturday.

On the afternoon I found out about the murder, I was in morose contemplation of my latest paycheck from the shop where I worked, destined to become $0.00 as the store gradually closed for all but pick-up and mail orders. There was a time when I would have shrugged off the disappearance of my retail income. It was just a side hustle after all, a way to safeguard my savings until the next travel gig. But come March, I was living in dread of the inevitable notice that my summer contract in Indonesia was off.

Most international education companies had already suspended programming indefinitely. I tried to imagine what a temporary gig with Uber Eats would entail in my small corner of West Virginia, delivering greasy buckets of KFC to stoned river raft guides and trays of Wendy's Frosties to the senior living center.

"Just wanted to fill you in on a couple of things," Mom said, her call interrupting my gloom spiral. "I'm in the hospital parking lot. They won't let me inside." My blood turned to cold ultrasound jelly as I struggled to recall the reason for my parents' latest medical sortie. It felt like every week Dad was coming home with some freshly stitched incision, Mom struggling to open a new bottle of medication.

"Is Dad okay? I thought it was just an outpatient thing."

"Oh, he's fine," Mom trilled, "though I'm pretty pissed that I can't go inside. I really have to pee."

"Okay then what, Mom?" The woman could bury a lede like no one's business.

"Well, apparently they found a dead body down the road just past the Pritchard's old place. Some guy was murdered, burned, and dumped. Oh, and a bear got into the neighbor's kitchen. Seems like someone's not taking this social distancing thing seriously!" She laughed. I struggled to parse her news. A bear. And a body. A body. I had questions, but my mother was eager to hang up. She and my father were stopping by Olive Garden on the way home, dining restrictions be damned.

I sought Google. Yes, a body. A Maryland man, between the ages of twenty and forty, found that morning, March 18, after a phone call from a passing motorist reported suspicious activity. There were only three articles on the subject, all with the same minimal information, plus an alarming number of unrelated hits when I entered the search terms "murder," "body," and the name of my town. The body had been found in "a remote location." I thought of the eight-minute drive to a yoga class and a good latte from where the corpse was discovered.

I walked over to the paned glass door that looked out toward the woods and road. Were it not for the trees, I could have seen straight to where the body was found. Where the murderer had stood. I pulled on a jacket and walked to the end of the driveway to peer down the road. There were two dark SUVs nudged into the fence line across from the old orchard where our neighbors grazed their cattle. A man in a dark windbreaker with the look of a high school wrestling coach stepped over a snarl of old barbed wire fence. I'd stepped over it myself many times for a quiet stroll back through the woods.

By early afternoon, the cars were gone. "You wanna take a piece with you?" My dad offered when I announced my intention to go check things out. It was his habit to offer me the use of a sidearm on a nearly daily basis. (I have been instructed not to reveal where all of the guns in their house are hidden, but suffice it to say that if you reach for a tissue chez Mom and Dad, your fingertips are as likely to brush cold steel as Kleenex.) I waved off his offer with my customary eyeroll.

"Don't get murdered!" Mom chirped from her reading chair as I pulled the front door shut behind me. I belatedly wondered whether I was about to traumatize myself, to see something I could never forget. But something had happened right there, something that rent the fabric of the place where I grew up, and I couldn't not go.

43

Within minutes, I was at the section of trampled fence that I'd seen the officer traverse. There were deep tire tracks in the soft spring mud but no stakes or strips of police tape making a cat's cradle with the trees. I peered into the brush and saw the usual. Deer carcasses picked down to bones and felted hide by vultures, crushed beer cans and greasy fast food bags littered across blackberry brambles and fallen tree limbs, forming a vegetal trampoline across the forest floor. Every place looked like it could be the place, but there was nothing new that I could see from my vantage point and so I left.

In the days to come no additional information emerged, though I checked the local news outlets compulsively. The body had been left for a very short time, swiftly retrieved by the authorities, and the matter taken up by the FBI. I forced myself to stop combing the local news for updates on the case and started teaching myself to play the ukulele, bake sourdough, and stop touching my face.

As predicted, my Indonesia job disappeared and the hiring process for the contract I'd been pursuing for the following year ground to a halt. One by one, access points for the Appalachian Trail and local parks closed to discourage the stubborn tailgate party atmosphere that persisted even after the stay-at-home order was issued. The perimeter of my life drew in smaller and tighter until even being outside began to feel like treading a bald spot in the carpet. I walked the roads bounding the agricultural land around my parents' property, passing within feet of the crime scene again and again until it reverted to nothing more than a low place in the fence where people dumped trash and shoveled off roadkill.

Then, human remains and the clothing of an unknown person were found just off of the Appalachian Trail on a section I'd hiked almost weekly before the lockdown. There was little information offered beyond a list of items found along with the remains. This included a Virgin Mary pendant with an inscribed prayer: "O Mary, conceived without sin, pray for us who have recourse to thee."

I grew up with cautionary trail tales, some overblown legends and others shocking truths that were enough to deter me from hiking it myself until years of solo expeditions elsewhere cured my reticence. As an adult, hiking became a stand-in for travel between my contracts abroad, an antidote to restlessness and loneliness each time I transplanted my life. I'd found pieces of home here and there over the years, but the closest I'd come to that elusive feeling was in the woods. When the trails closed to prevent the spread of COVID-19, I stopped breathing quite so deeply. When I read about this latest death, that breath went shallower still.

A few days after hearing of the trail remains, I took a walk with my boyfriend near my parents' home. We decided to loop behind the patch of roadside woods where the body was found and through an old pear orchard. Walking this bit of forest and meadow felt necessary to stamp some familiarity back into the land with each step, scuffing away the stain of violence.

Cattle bones that looked like something Fred Flintstone would pitch into the yard for Dino littered our path as our footfalls kept startling a massive herd of deer from one browsing area to the next. We shimmied under fence wire and poked around the stone ruins of an old house. It was an aimless, contented outing but also a defiance of the way people tended to move through spaces tainted by violence – swiftly, arms sealed tight to soft sides, eyes locked on the ground.

At the close of our loop, we approached the road again and followed the fence line back to our starting point. Mid-step, my boyfriend startled, teetering for a moment as if at a cliff's edge. We'd stumbled right up to the border of a patch of charred ground roughly the size an adult would leave if he'd fallen into a snowdrift and made an angel. My throat convulsed in a hard, hydraulic action. Seeing the burned ground made the body real. Heat flared in my chest and eyes. With the pandemic shrinking my world by the day, the land left for me to walk had become an extension of my body. I did not want my body to feel the way that patch of ground looked, ruined and forgotten.

The next day I returned to the site and sat beside the ashes in hopes that my silent witnessing might fade the dark imprint of what had happened there. I poked a wild turkey feather into the ash along with a stick of lit incense. As I sat, afternoon sunlight crept over the charred ground, turning the smoke from the incense into dancers entwined. When I finally rose and walked away, I felt lighter, like my body had declared a kind of truce with itself.

Two days later, I was out in the yard when my mother called to me from the back deck. "There's an update on the murder," she said, then rattled off a series of grisly details. One particular phrase – "He was alive when they brought him here" – sent me bolting up the steps to my apartment to read the full coverage online.

There had been an argument in an apartment across the state line in Maryland. A man was stabbed, wounded but not killed, tied up and brought to the spot beyond the barbed wire fence. A confusing element to the story had been how someone driving down the road in the dim morning light could notice an inert form thirty feet into the woods. As it happened, the murderer set fire to the body after dealing the victim a lethal blow to the head. The flames were the "suspicious activity" that caught the passing motorist's eye and drew him into the woods. So it wasn't only the disposal of a body but the act of taking and desecrating a life that occurred within a few minutes' walk from my door. No distance at all, really, from where a man was murdered as I slept.

Nothing has made this quarantine feel more real to me than losing access to the wild places I seek out to remember the size of the world, and nothing has taught me more about the fiction of distance than the violent death of a stranger right there. I think about this all the time now, the juxtaposition of distance and immediacy that defines what it means to be the resident of a place where a person was killed, and the citizen of a planet where death-by-virus stalks on silent feet. A world in which everything is too far away and far too close all at the same time.

Consider the Elbow

Shelly Gill Murray
55, Minnesota, United States

I stare at the Porta-Potty, sizing it up like a formidable opponent. After a three-mile run around the lake, I couldn't make it home without stopping here. A woman approaches and although she says, "You waiting to use that?" Her face says the rest: *I do not want your sweaty ass giving me COVID-19. Let me go first!*

"Go ahead," I say, moving into observation phase. I watch her fling the door open, COVID-19 vapors wafting out like helium balloons released at a birthday party.

Why did I leave my mask in the car?

She uses her back to brace against the door's spring hinges as she enters. I hear the lock slide over and the seat squeak, the third of what I calculated to be three hands-on maneuvers. After a moment, the toilet paper rattles and then the toilet seat slams down. Touch number four.

I can skip that step – who puts the fucking lid down anyway?

Damn all the men who could get the job done with no contact, wouldn't even need to shut the door!

I hear her pumping the hand sanitizer. Touch number five. But essential. The door latch clicks open and she appears, forearm leading the way. She looks at me as if to say, *Are you still here?* She jogs away.

Okay, there has to be a way to do this.

Siri, how do you use a Porta-Potty without touching it?

The elbow is the key, I decide, but first I need my foot. I stick my big toe under the corner of the door and pivot to the left pulling it open while I tuck my elbow in and step inside. Two touches eliminated! I use the same elbow to slide the lock over, then turn and belittle the woman who came before me for shutting the toilet lid.

Am I really going to lower my torso toward that putrid seat to hook my elbow under it? Will I fall off balance and add more touches if I try to lift my toe that high?

Elbow it is.

Staring at the toilet seat, I remember fondly the YMCA where I used to work out before the pandemic. For years I complained about the pain of doing squats with 40 pounds on my back, knees screaming. It suddenly occurred to me all those squats were for this one moment. In *A Prayer for Owen Meany*, Owen practiced a jump shot thousands of times as a kid and used it as an adult to save orphans from a grenade explosion in an airport bathroom. The desperate move cost him his hands. I am the Owen Meany of Porta-Potty. I'll save myself and countless others from COVID-19 all because I practiced a silly exercise that I wasn't sure I had a use for. I can now hover in a squat for several minutes, quads be damned.

Finished with my business, I'm in the home stretch. Skip the lid, elbow the hand sanitizer, and keep a little for the elbow. Elbow the lock over, hip-check the door, and suck in a breath of fresh air. I congratulate myself on being an architect of wonderment. Then I glance at the woman waiting nearby, toddlers in tow.

"Consider the elbow," I say, and walk away.

Positive

Storey Clayton

40, West Virginia, United States

On the night we discovered your existence, your mother and I held each other in the bathroom. We danced in the adjacent bedroom, then again in the kitchen. We laughed and cried and smiled and shook our heads in wonder. We changed for dinner, a fancy dinner we ordered in at home, because we couldn't go out. It was April 8, 2020, and there was a global pandemic.

On the night we discovered your existence, your mother peed in a cup, dipped a stick, and left the room, a ritual we'd practiced for a handful of months: January, February, March. Those times, tears of frustration, mutterings of disappointment, a week or more of waiting for the right moment to pee, to have a chance, the moment pregnant with anticipation but nothing more. *What if we can't?* The unspoken worry we shared. The image of a future where we visited aquariums and Pixar movies and county fairs alone to gaze longingly at families loomed on a foggy horizon.

Just days before April 8th, she'd turned to me in bed, alarmed, reading a news story on her phone, weeks into a semi-sequester we were calling lockdown. We'd abandoned restaurants, movie theaters, visits with friends, seeing only the grocery store or a nearby trail over a thick cloth mask. "Do you think we should stop?" she asked. "With the pandemic? Things are getting out of control."

"Stop?" I said.

"Well, pause. Not forever. Just until things calm down. Stabilize."

"Maybe," I said, thinking of a birth in a hospital overrun with dying patients. A hospital like in Wuhan, where the virus had first become an outbreak. I pictured you born in a hallway, a parking lot, maybe even at home. "But we may be waiting a long time."

We had already waited a long time. A five-year courtship capped by ten months of engagement flowing into two and a half years of marriage. Nearly a decade of practice as a couple, almost all of it under a shared roof, to get to the point where we could say, yes, we are ready for this. We are ready for you.

Were we always ready? I think we always knew it would be us, it would be you. There was a time eight years before, just a year in, when we were standing in a 24-hour Walgreens aisle in East Brunswick, New Jersey at 3:38 in the morning, the fluorescent light turning your normally pallid mother vampiric as she started to fret. Her hand was on a fateful pink box and she turned to look up at me, shivering in my wet shoes, and ask what would happen, what we would do. "What if?" she said.

And I turned and grabbed her hands and said "If it's positive, it will be hard. It will be scary. It will take a lot of work and time and energy we don't feel we have right now. But in a little less than nineteen years, you and I will be sitting at a high school graduation and we will look at each other just like I'm looking at you now and we'll be so glad, so grateful, that it was positive tonight."

She looked at the floor, a sickly stained carpet. Then at me, square in the eyes. "Promise?"

"Promise." By then I knew it would be us, it would be you.

It wasn't that night, of course. It was negative. Your mother was only twenty, a year younger than when her mother got the positive result that became your mother. It would be you, but not yet.

On the night we discovered your existence, your mother flopped on the bed, facedown, and tried to tell herself that it would be fine if it was negative, better really, because of the pandemic, because things were bound to get worse, because we didn't know what would happen with healthcare and her job and we had to move in a year when I finished my graduate program and we could always save more money first, shouldn't we do that instead? We could always have more money. It was bound to be easier later. She looked up at me. "Any of this sound convincing?"

"Nope," I admitted.

"Yeah, me neither."

And the timer went off, a staccato chime on her phone, and she sent me in and I asked if she was sure she wanted me to look first and she said yes, it's fine, go ahead. And I stepped into the small bathroom, over the threshold where the carpet met linoleum, separated by a little strip of golden metal. My eyes found the plastic rod, flat and white and plastic and blending into the white formica countertop surrounding the white ceramic sink. Twin blue lines, thin and parallel, faintly disrupted the icy surface.

I hesitated. "Two lines, right? That's what we're looking for?"

"Two lines."

"It's two lines."

Her sockfeet pounded into the bathroom, she hip-checked me away from where I leaned over the sink. "Oh my God, it's two lines!"

"We're having a baby."

"We're having a baby!"

We took pictures. She took another test, and then another, which I chided her about, her short dark brown hair up in a messy ponytail as I patted it, grinning broadly. "I think the lines are getting darker," she insisted. I rolled my eyes and laughed and suggested we dress up for dinner, take pictures to celebrate. "We can't tell anyone yet!" she said.

"Not for the world. For us. For them," I pointed at her belly button, still nestled deep in the flat of her stomach.

She agreed and selected her favorite old black-and-white striped dress, the one she wore most often to debate tournaments when we were dating, a tasteful cut above the knees, short sleeves, a V-neck showing off her collarbones. I chose the suit I married her in, dark teal, from Britain, with a light blue-green shirt the color of my eyes and a lavender tie with gray spots she'd bought me years before. On the way to the kitchen for hasty awkward selfies, I grabbed the onesie we'd bought at a Target in New Orleans just after our wedding, the one we couldn't pass up, the quiet pledge, the down payment on the future. It is turquoise and displays inquisitive white cartoon rabbits and small yellow chicks and sports the phrase *every bunny loves me* on a small patch where a chest pocket would go. Our house rabbit looked on in curiosity, wondering at the noise we made, the jubilant commotion unusual for a Wednesday night.

On the night we discovered your existence, we took pictures and ate takeout Indian food from the best restaurant in Morgantown, West Virginia. We forgot, for an evening, about the emerging pandemic and lockdown and the impending election and my school and her work and our past. We grinned goofily and talked loudly and thought about just one small part of our future, small but so much more important than anything we'd done before.

On the night we discovered your existence, you were already so loved.

Primal Scream

Sumitra Mattai
39, New York, United States

I unleashed my first primal scream in April 2020. New York City's stay-at-home orders were mandated the week my maternity leave would have ended, extending my time at home with my four-month-old daughter, Zadie, and five-year-old son, Miles. I read the news on my phone while I nursed Zadie every few hours, my body tense, bracing against the apocalypse. I forced myself not to cry as I tied my first home sewn mask over Miles's face, his dark eyes full of questions I couldn't answer. In my blurred state, the pandemic felt like a paranoid delusion, a sick joke on a whole generation.

The day of my first scream, Zadie was protesting a nap. This was not unusual; she fought against sleep day and night. But that afternoon, her cries were like sandpaper rubbing against my sanity, threadbare as a scrap of gauze. All I wanted to do was drink a cup of coffee and stare at a wall for an hour. But Zadie's voice clawed the air, her chubby arms flailing out of her swaddle. At that moment, I snapped. I made a sound I had never made before in thirty-nine-years of existence, a feral release of frustration, rage, and fear, a cannonball of a sound that skinned and scraped my throat.

Needless to say, this visceral noise did not comfort Zadie, who only wailed harder. Miles ran into the room, and immediately began bawling. Soon we were all crying in shock and confusion. I don't remember what happened next. Probably I put on a movie, and we huddled on the couch for two hours, watching Lightning McQueen almost win his Piston Cup for the hundredth time. I remember apologizing to Miles, who listened with a faraway expression as I tried to explain how my emotions staged a coup and took control of me.

With my second scream, I felt it coming, rising from deep in my gut, like a need to vomit. I ran outside to let the sound rip its way out of my throat. Apparently, I would rather scare my neighbors than my children.

Between the first two screams and the next two screams, I broke a stool, a white plastic IKEA stool Miles stepped on to reach the bathroom sink. I raised it over my head and brought it down hard on the ground, again and again until the plastic legs cracked.

Looking back on it now, I know empirically what brought on this behavior – the panic and uncertainty of the coronavirus combined with the crippling exhaustion of a newborn. I can only vaguely remember the incidents that set me off – Zadie refusing to sleep, a quote from Trump, the first of many work Zoom calls in which the CEO offered platitudes like, "the sun will come out tomorrow."

My stress was nothing compared to the stress of so many. I was inessential, a temporary stay-at-home mom in a safe home. But creature comforts could not stop the full tilt of an existential crisis.

I had a therapist and a meditation app, but my feelings were too big and chaotic to process in the usual ways. Death loomed, and I raged.

Flames

Ebony Macfarlane
26, New South Wales, Australia

"Is this weird?" I asked no one in particular, as we settled on the cliffside. Everyone laughed. No one bothered to answer properly. Of course it was weird. We were sitting with take away pizzas and beers, overlooking the valley. We'd done this many times before.

Across the canyon, angry red smoke billowed up the side of the plateau. Glowing red lines highlighted the side of the cliff and made strange patterns. That was the unfamiliar part. The main fire looked like a steam engine hurtling through the bush, smoke surrounding it and trailing behind.

I was sort of used to bushfires by now, having lived in the Blue Mountains my whole life. We had been living with the threat for a while. I was even used to them this fire season, with two burning nearby for weeks. Monitoring the Fires Near Me app had become part of the daily routine. I had already left work early one day to help my parents prepare to evacuate their home. My partner's parents had evacuated and then been able to return. But this one was closest to home.

When I got off work that day, I had messages, calls, and notifications telling me that the fire had started. My partner, two friends, and I organized our cliffside rendezvous. Here we were, sitting and overlooking our valley. It was breathtaking, as usual. But today for very different reasons.

The fire made its way up the side of the plateau swiftly. Small spot fires splintered off the main fire front. They left strangely dazzling patterns on the cliff side. At this time of day, normally the sun would be hitting the right spot to perfectly illuminate the rock face. Today, the sky behind the plateau was grey and somber. It was mesmerizing. It reminded me of a macabre form of entertainment from the dark ages. I couldn't look away.

It's odd, the way we like to watch destructive things. When my partner's parents were forced to evacuate, they stood on the big bridge over the highway in their suburb. A crowd had formed up there, watching the smoke cloud that may or may not have been devouring their properties. Watching and silently cheering for the helicopter that flew overhead, collecting water and dropping it on the fire.

There was a helicopter here now. The red helper in the sky was another familiar sight. The fires still burning close to the North and South of us felt like they had started an eternity ago. One long month of warnings and evacuation notices lighting up our phones. We watched as the helicopter dropped a balloon of water on the fire, did a circle and flew back over our heads to get more water. I wondered where they got it from. I had heard that people with a pool or dam could volunteer for their water to be used to fight fires. Maybe that's where the fighter was getting it. There wasn't much water in natural places lately, and certainly not down there amongst our burning bushwalking tracks. The helicopter flew back over us, headed toward the fire. It looked tiny as it flew into the black and red blur, a David against Goliath.

Someone mused whether it was a single person in the helicopter. We had heard how thinly the fire fighters were stretched. How terrifying it must be to willingly fly into a fire front. A lone soldier against an angry beast, intent on engulfing and annihilating. The water wasn't having any observable effect on the fire. Nonetheless, the helicopter continued to make the round trip again and again.

Someone's phone sounded. The Fires Near Me app was notifying us of the upgrading status of the fire. By now, it had made its way entirely up the wall and was atop the plateau, burning towards the adjacent valley. It had an insatiable appetite. I thought of the trees and animals being devoured. I thought of the properties it was approaching. Colleagues and their families lived down there. A friend kept her horse there.

One of the group suggested the pub. I felt just as strange about leaving as I felt sitting there watching. This year, we had learned not to question all that much. We would wait to find out what happened. As we drove back along the highway toward Katoomba town center, a handwritten sign caught my eye: *Thank you firies.*

I thought of the lone helicopter battling over the valley.

Texas Predators

Jose Francisco Fonseca
35, Texas, United States

Oil became cheaper than dirt. Ignacio, Ralphy, and I, are sitting under the cottonwood tree that has dressed itself with a bit of chain link fence. The rest of the backyard fence sits firm and tight, resisting morning glory vines that try to drag it down. Ralphy's red pickup has its hood up, and we have the power-steering pump, hose, air duct, and fuel rail scattered on a blue tarp, a black liquid mix of gas and soot pooling under every motor part. That same black liquid mix streaks down our forearms and covers are hands. The smell of gas is strong, and makes the Coors I am drinking taste weird.

"There has to be some mistake," Ignacio says. "How the hell is oil not making money?"

"There's too much of it," Ralphy says. "The fucking Arabs and Russians pumped out too much."

"*Cabrón.*"

"It's this fake virus. Everyone has bought the lie and it's sending everything to shit. Fucking mainstream media."

"*Cabrón*."

"Once Trump wins again, this whole fucking mess will be fixed by him. You'll see."

"You think he will win?" I ask.

"I don't see why he wouldn't," Ralphy says, "there are more Republicans inside the country than out in the coasts."

"You sound like it's guaranteed, like a sunset."

"It is," Ralphy says, "it has to be."

We sit in silence while we take our swigs of Coors. The smell of gasoline that fogs my mouth is washed away temporarily with a bitter, crisp taste. The cool liquid hits my stomach and every bone in my body loosens from the muscle tissue. It is a bit strange to sit in silence here in Ralphy's backyard. There is an oil pump nearby, and you could hear that thing day and night for the last three years creaking as its head and neck bobbed constantly. Its wheel churring in a blur, its belt streaking. Now that belt and wheel are cemented in place, the neck and head still.

"Well this motor isn't going to put itself together," Ralphy says.

"I'm going to the Allsups to get some cigs," I say. "Should I buy another six pack?"

"Here," Ignacio hands me a twenty. "Keep the change."

"*Gracias, güey*," I say.

"*Es nada*," Ignacio says, "as long as I can bum some cigs."

"*Claro*."

The town around has begun to crawl to a standstill. The road I drive on has a few drowsy cars passing by. No more dusty roughnecks coming in from the fields with new 350s to buy groceries at Lowes, or to get drunk and dumb after buying a twelve pack at Stripes. I see a single teal semi-truck with no trailer make its way slowly across an intersection in front of me. No more semi-trucks lumbering around the town on the loop, like chrome sharks circling a bleeding whale. The radio plays Ramón Ayala's "Baraja de Oro," his rough raspy voice tumbling out over his drunk accordion. No more talk from the mayor and the oil companies of decade-long prosperity, now pink slips and cutbacks. A familiar cycle here, but when you get high off the fumes of the oil being pumped out, you tend to forget the mirage this place truly is.

Across the street from the crimson brick courthouse, in front of the large gray brick Baptist church, is the bronze and oxidized green sculpture of three roughnecks leaning on one another, wearing their helmets and overalls. My abuelo, Kiko Morales, got land in this mirage. The first "Mexican" to work as a roustabout for the deceased Penbrook Oil Company. He was born a Tejano, not Mexicano, but to the all-white crew at the time there was no distinction. That all changed when he started working though, his brown skin and their white skin sweating, burning in the sun, getting covered in the black blood when a pipe burst. All their bones bending and rubbing roughly under that skin, sharing the grit of dirt in their teeth when a dust storm slammed in. Feeling their stomachs rumble with hunger whenever the boom turned to bust on the rusting hinge that is the economy. I like to think that one of the three men in the statue is my abuelo, helping to hold the distributed weight.

I fumble for my red bandana when I get to the Allsups. I put it on bandito style and walk toward the front door. Inside I see the young girl wearing a painter's mask. She is texting and doesn't lift her eyes as the bell on the door jingles. I get my beer from behind some foggy glass and head back to the cashier to buy the Camels black box she has behind her. The sheriff is there, his khaki uniform nice and crisp stretches over his large belly, his white cowboy hat dusty. He is wearing a red bandana also and looks at me with ice blue eyes as I walk up.

"Jose, is that you *muchacho*?" The sheriff asks with his thick Texas accent.

"Yes sir," I answer, "came in to buy some drinks and smokes."

"Jesus, y'all Mexicans look alike now. Makes my life a bit harder."

"Is it because people are robbing stores more because they masked up?"

"Hell no. Everyone has a gun here, plus there is nothing to rob. Not anymore anyways. It just makes it hard to keep track of the Gutierrezes. Them damn boys always causing trouble."

"Well sir, I can tell you that Ignacio is causing no trouble. He is helping me and Ralphy change out fuel injectors on his pick up."

The cashier hands the sheriff a log of Grizzly chew. He tilts his hat at the cashier and points at me with the log.

"Jose," the sheriff says, "you have a good day now. And no drinking any of them Coors while you drive. I know you Mexicans love to toss a few while you cruise around town."

"Have a good day, sir," I answer. "Don't go crashing into the post office. Y'all country cops tend to doze off while your car is not in park."

The sheriff laughed. "Doc should have never given that boy them painkillers. He would still have a job today."

On my drive back to Ralphy's the town has revived a bit. There are a few more cars and trucks trudging along, the high school boys inside the vehicles shouting out to one another, revving engines or turning up the music in their cars. Some have black bars over their cheeks, some have headbands on. They all have sweaty faces and grass stains on their arms and faces. I see Ignacio's youngest brother taunting a kid on his bike from his old white Toyota, the other boys in the car laughing. The kid on his bike has on his football pants and cleats. As they speed away, Ignacio's youngest brother tosses a plastic Coke bottle at the kid, spilling Coke all over him. They drive off to futures that look dusty and brittle, like a tumbleweed rolling along a cracked, potholed highway.

When I get to Ralphy's I see the white sheriff truck parked next to Ignacio's bent up blue truck. Walking up to the tree dressed with chain link fence, where we all were sitting before, I see the sheriff with his cowboy hat off, sitting on the yellow Yeti cooler. His hair is thin and gray, slicked back pressing hard on his head. He smiles broadly with Ignacio and Ralphy.

"The man of the hour has arrived," Ralphy says. "What took you so long?"

"I was talking to him," I answer, pointing to the sheriff.

"How the hell did I make it here quicker than you?" The sheriff asks. "We were like three minutes apart. You Mexicans move as slow as you work."

"How much moving you doing," Ignacio says, "with a *pansa* as big as yours?"

"This *pansa*," the sheriff answers, "is the result of steak dinners from a wife that happened to be the high school prom queen and drinking plenty of good beer. Speaking of which, start passing those along before they get warmer."

"Jose, I heard you ratted me out to *pansón* over here."

"He asked about you," I say, "said it was hard to keep track of the Gutierrez boys."

"You all look alike," the Sheriff says, "you Mexicans, I mean."

"It's not our fault that we are handsome bastards compared to you *güeros*," Ralphy says. "No wonder your daughter is in my house right now scrapping up some beans and pork chops for us."

"She never had no good sense or taste, but her pork chops taste just like her mother's. And those have a good taste."

All four of us sit there as the sky turns from slate to gray to black. A splatter of stars threatens to drip on us in thick inky fluid. The tree rattles from some crows that have made a nest in it. Their caws drowned out by our laughter. When Ralphy's wife calls us in for the pork chops we slowly make our way to the orange light of the kitchen, stepping around the truck parts on the blue tarp. I hear the chain link rattle behind me, and when I turn around I see three sets of eyes looking back at me. I can't tell if they are dogs or coyotes, but I can just make out the outline of four legs and stiff tails. They keep looking at me, at the house, trying to figure us out.

"If you ever do," I say, "then please tell me."

Rose-Colored in Retrospect

Kendall Beck
16, Illinois, United States

The blue light from my phone lit up my face as I scrolled, leaning on my kitchen counter. I mindlessly filed through my photo app and watched as the dates turned back in time. I slowed my scroll and tapped on a video. Mine and my friend's faces flashed on the screen. I remembered the day exactly:

The wind gently blew my hair into my eyes. I tucked my flyaways behind my ear and watched as my friend lifted her hand to do the same. My seventh period History teacher's voice echoed in the back of my mind.

Perched atop my car, I hugged my knees to my chest. "It's so strange that we won't be in school for two weeks."

My friend turned to listen. A dazed expression danced across her face but disappeared into denial with the furrowing of her brows. "My dad wonders if it will last longer than that. Some companies have sent their employees to work from home until the summer. I'm not sure what will happen to us," she trailed off and looked down at her hands. Even in the dimming light I could see her dark brown eyes, serious yet curious.

We both turned to face west, the periwinkle night before us. It felt right to return to one of our favorite spots: the open-air top level of the city's parking garage. A touch of coral colored the clouds. They made their descent below the buildings in the distance. Besides the rustle of the breeze and the muffled music escaping from the open skylight below us, the night was silent.

My friend broke the silence first, shrugging her shoulders dismissively. "I guess I don't see how this could affect much more than two weeks. We'll be right back to finish the year."

With my left fist clutching my shirt sleeve I wiped my watery eyes. Spring arrived, but the wind was still harsh and wet. "I hope you're right." The shakiness in my voice surprised me. I tightened my fingers around my crossed arms and breathed deep. "After these two weeks it'll be spring break, and then we'll start preparing for finals —"

"Which wouldn't be the worst to miss," she giggled. Neither of us said anything for a couple minutes and stared ahead at the darkening sky. I shifted in place, leaning my hands behind me to prop myself up. As the periwinkle turned to a slate gray before us, the silver crescent of the moon shone brighter above our heads.

"Friday the thirteenth," I whispered into the breeze.

"Everything feels weird today. Look at the streets." I followed my friend's gaze to the empty grid below us. The traffic lights blinked, changing every fourteen seconds, despite the absence of an audience. Green. Yellow. Red.

"Don't you want to remember this moment?" My friend pulled her phone out from her pocket and tapped the camera. "Everyone is talking about how we're 'history in the making.' We should film something to show our kids."

I nodded and scooted into view, anticipating the video would make its way into the yearly montage my friend creates each Christmas. Her thumb tapped "Record" and the button's steady red began to pulse.

We finished the video and I slid down into the driver's seat. "I never imagined history-making could be so uncertain."

My friend followed behind me. "It's always rose-colored in retrospect."

I studied our faces on the screen. We looked young. Or maybe just happy. I rested my chin in my hand and hit play on the video.

"Hi! It's us. It's Friday, March 13th, 2020, and we were just let out of school for a two week break because of the coronavirus."

My voice cut in.

"Maybe you're watching this because you're our kids. Or you're us in the future. Anyway, it's super disorienting. No one knows what to do. It seems the whole world doesn't either. But we thought we would make a video! Hopefully things are different when you're watching this."

I pressed pause then clicked the power button. My reflection in the dark screen made my heart flutter. A tear escaped and dribbled down my left cheek.

Rose-colored in retrospect.

Emancipation by Quarantine

Danielle Joffe
55, Connecticut, United States

Men have always had opinions about my hair — long, short, dyed, or in braids.

My papa, who was almost bald, set me upon a chair in his living room when I was four. He trimmed my long straight chestnut bangs and then the length, a little bit here, a little more there, doing his best to demonstrate his prowess with his black handled steel office scissors and a fine plastic comb. Instead, he finally called the job done when my blonde chignon-coiffed mother arrived and screamed to see her perfect little girl now clad in a crooked "boy's bowl cut."

The man I call Dad loved my braids, two long plaits that I wore with overalls and mosquito bites on visiting day at summer camp when I was nine and met him for the first time. When I was 17 and boldly cut my mane from waist length to shoulders, his eyes grew round and he gasped, "What did you do?!" I turned tail to my room and cried.

My first husband, who proudly drove a battered one-ton crew cab pick-up truck named Brownie and believed in free love, preferred my hair long and told me so. He liked how it brushed across his skin when we had sex.

Later, my after-the-divorce, way-too-old-for-me boyfriend sent me to dye my roots and get highlights. He told me, as he gently kissed the corners of my mouth, that when the time was right, a little filler here or there would be just the thing.

And now my ever-practical German-born husband thinks I would look just great if I just chopped it into a spunky pixie cut.

It's been months since I was in a salon. In the shower, I explore with unmanicured fingers, the full length of my hair, past my shoulders, all the way down to the paintbrush ends. I follow a memory to the last time it took two fists to squeeze out the water and listen to it slap the tile floor:

I am 31 and sitting splayed on the Navajo-carpeted floor of my living room in Santa Fe. My hair is loose and falls forward to form a private tent for just me and my two-month-old baby girl, Sophia, who is lying on her back and cooing up at me. The two of us stare into each other's eyes, lost in an intimate infinite revelry. "Who are you?" I wonder out loud. "Who will you become?" She grabs a fist full of my hair and tries to stuff it in her mouth.

And now at 55, dripping wet, I approach the mirror and peer at my reflection. I examine the silvery radial expanse that sprouts outward from my scalp and exposes a part of myself I have tried in vain to keep captive. Against my will, I am unadorned. Three months of gray hair, naked and on display.

I decide right then and there. I like it. And a thought occurs to me that I never allowed before. What if I stop painting my hair the color of youth, chasing other people's images of sexy, and obeying the rules that tell me to cover up, be quiet, and conceal the truth of my years?

For too long, I have obediently pursued fabricated fantasies of pretty, sexy, and young; my hair the unwitting proof of compliance and willingness to be wanted, while under the dye, my abdicated self mutely waited. For the first time I allow myself to acknowledge and even claim this part of myself that has been hidden for years under chemical covers.

And now my husband appears on his side of the vanity to examine his blond head which has grown out of its well-behaved trim corporate cut. "You should grow it out," I tell him, "It would look so sexy!"

Melt

Nathan Holic
41, Florida, United States

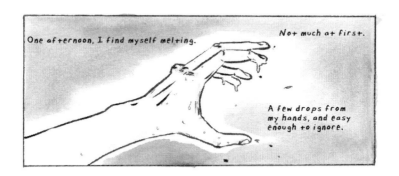

It wasn't so long ago that I was wearing pants everyday, button—downs, belts. Now, it's all tshirts and shorts, and they're plucked from piles in the bathroom that I hope are clean.

I've forgotten what it even feels like to pull something off a hanger.

The dripping.

I try not to notice, but it's like a pebble in my shoe.

Just little drops, a nuisance, but it won't stop.

And only me to see it.

Easy enough to clean the drips, I suppose.

Not any worse than the bedhead that I half assed comb out.

Home is my office. Home is my life, and my life is home. I have all the time in the world to clean.

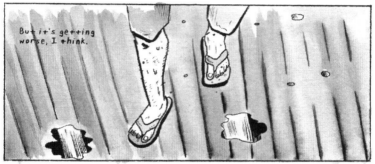

But it's getting worse, I think.

Awhile back, when everyone was panic buying every damn cleaning product, I stocked up on Swiffer pads, more than I'll use in five years. The puddles are oily, but they're no match for the power of corporate ingenuity.

My floors are cleaner than they've ever been, really. Ready for guests, but I haven't spoken to anyone in forever, don't even remember how.

More drips today than yesterday.

More yesterday than the day before.

It runs into my eyes, into my ears. I want to dab with a towel, wipe my forehead, but if I wipe away the melt, will anything even remain?

Sometimes it seems to stop.

Sometimes it's a cool morning, and it's sunny, and I think maybe everything's all right again.

My clothes melt with me, but not the mask. The mask always stays.

I'm alone in my house, but still I wear the mask so that there will be one piece of me left intact.

Some days I want to wear the mask on my Zoom meeting, too.

Other days, when the melt is bad, I mute my video, never offer any opinions even when I've got so much to say...

My voice gurgles. Everyone has to hear it, right?

If only the computer would melt. Dissolving from the top down, the mouse becoming a puddle under my fingertips.

But there's no hope of that. Even when I'm gone entirely, the computer will be here.

The things we want to see melt away will always be just fine.

I don't know.

For now, this is all there is.

Part III: Summer

Going Gently

Ed Davis
70, Ohio, United States

The call, when it comes on July 28, draws me from bed, as I always knew it would.

"I just checked on your mother and she's not responsive." A pause. "She's already cold."

The word cold will haunt me later. Right now I'd like to know — is she dead? However, I'm accustomed to contradictions and partial answers from those who've cared for my mother at the nursing home where she has lived for over thirty years. If indeed it's the end, it's been a long time coming. There'd been a false alarm several years before, and I'd sped from my home in southeastern Ohio to southern West Virginia to make it in time. On the way, a doctor called to inform me my mother had aspirated and might not make it. But she did, and I got to stay by her side in the ICU. I'm about to ask for clarification when the aide adds:

"We'll call you back as soon as the doctor gets here."

I resign myself to waiting a little longer to know for sure.

But the call, that chilling word – cold – has increased my stress level to twelve on a ten-point scale, paralyzing me while my wife arises, commiserates, and we slowly begin our morning routines. But before I've brushed my teeth, I know it might be too late to prevent...but I can't let myself imagine.

Decades ago, my mom, mentally ill all her life, had signed a form before witnesses at the home saying she wanted all measures taken to save her life. Now I imagine the "heroic measures" of a full code on my glass-fragile, 90-pound mom. I'm horrified by the thought that her body might be assaulted in her last moments on earth. Not my mom, sufferer of schizophrenia for at least the past two decades; who'd done the best she could for me after my father fled for good when I was in fourth grade; who, while she could've considered me a burden, gave me unconditional love. It is my moment to show her the same.

I must act quickly, but before I can, the phone rings again. It's the hospice nurse. "They're taking her to Bluefield Community. The ambulance is on the way."

Thank God I enlisted hospice services months earlier. Fingers trembling, I call the hospital receptionist who transfers me to the ER nurse. I explain shakily the directive and entreat her, as I did with all the other authorities, to reconsider. Now here it comes: the same explanation I've gotten for the past several years. It can't legally be undone.

But the nurse doesn't say that. She says she'll talk to the attending physician and call me back.

Even though I'm heartened a bit, the wait is hell. This is the culmination of mine and my society's terrible failure. I'd talked to a lot of sympathetic folks, including government agencies, trying to rescind the directive she'd made when, clearly not of sound mind (she'd never been of sound mind in my lifetime), she'd signed that form. We'd let her choose the least humane option, not imagining the nightmare scenario ahead, clueless that my then-robust mom would live to be 93 and become a shell of her former feisty self.

Since then, I'd rationalized that she would die peacefully in her sleep — isn't that what we all hope for our parents (for ourselves)? Which is no excuse. In front of witnesses, I should've been of sound enough mind to have explained clearly, patiently, lovingly, what she was signing. It would've been hard for a lot of reasons. Would I be seen as trying to deny my mom's right to have her last wishes honored? Did I want to refuse her the same health care everyone should be entitled to? The outcome might've been the same, but I could've tried. Things might be different for my beloved mother, for myself, right now.

As minutes pass, I recall how quickly she declined, following the illness that landed her in ICU years earlier (one of so many illnesses, falls and accidents that I've forgotten what happened that time). Gradually I realized she no longer recognized me. I still kissed her cheek, held her hand and spoke to her, disciplining myself not to ask questions she could no longer answer, though she tried, usually just repeating my words. Dementia? Worsening schizophrenia? It didn't matter. The last remaining fragments of her mind, weakening for so long, had seemingly dissolved. For at least the last two years, I knew I'd been visiting her body, her mind long fled. Surprisingly I accepted it, almost as if I were visiting her grave. Almost. I still held her hand and it always felt warm.

My phone rings, ending my reverie. It's the ER physician on duty returning my call. "Mr. Davis, since you expressed your wish to the nurse, along with me, that's two witnesses. We'll fill out the DNR form so it's ready before your mother arrives."

I'm suddenly ablaze in light. All my worry has come down to the decision of compassionate, reasonable human beings. I would hug these medical heroes, including the hospice nurse, if they were present – virus be damned.

"Thank you," I breathe.

Before noon, the doctor calls to say Mom has passed peacefully. My mental image now morphs from the horror of the full code to my mother's withered, still body contained between clean, crisp sheets awaiting transport by Seaver Mortuary to her home town ten miles away. I am grateful now that her sister connected me with Seaver two decades ago to "take care of everything." They do. Geographical distance as well as the immeasurable existential distance caused by the pandemic means that I am entirely dependent on the kindness of professionals in my native state – folks whose Appalachian accents used to be mine. Not strangers now, not fellow West Virginians; somehow, they are kin.

A Human Was Here

Haitham Dinnawi
30, Beirut, Lebanon

It took me a full six days to begin processing the chaos with so much death and destruction in 30 seconds.

I was on my way to pick up my mom from work when the blast happened. Everything shook. I called my wife at home to check up on her, then rushed to my mother, got her and went back home to see what the blast was. Less than 24 hours later, we rushed to pick up the dead and the injured, not fully understanding what had happened. We answered the silent calls for help, too shocked to cry, too angry and tired. A mix of emotions each overpowering the other, I couldn't even tell which one I was experiencing at any given point in time.

There was an obvious need to document what was happening, and relay it to the rest of the world. I was roaming the streets with a broom and my camera. Taking photos, helping here and there, just doing anything possible.

At that moment, I began to slowly realize the gravity and damage, and I broke down.

The port was to my left as I stood on Charles Helou bridge, and to my right, a bus. It was mangled from the blast – there was nothing to absorb the shockwave – glass shattered everywhere with blood stains all over the outside and the inside. I leaned into the crumbled figure, took my photo, and that's when it hit me.

The scenario in this bus played over and over in my head.

The chaos.

There was nothing between them and the blast.

Where were they going? What were they all feeling? Could you imagine the panic in this bus?

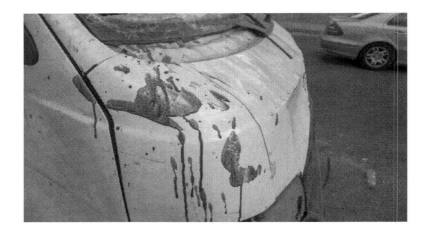

I broke down.

I had gone through the seven stages of grief and back to square one, back to where I started. I didn't have the luxury to heal. None of us did.

Especially after we lost over 200 people. Especially after we had over dozens still missing.

Especially after having 7,000 injured.

Especially after we had 300,000 displaced from their homes.

Especially after a big portion of the city was decimated and eradicated. Or we had to consider the looming threat over the last 9 months of losing your job, or not being able to withdraw your hard-earned money, or aimlessly calling for change, or – or...

In front of all the obstacles, and challenges, oppression, bad luck, negligence, terrorism, warfare, conspiracy or whatever you want to call it, the Lebanese people were still there and I had to do my duty: Show the world what has happened to Lebanon, and help rebuild in any means possible.

Pandemic Madness

Paul Silvester
60, Hampshire, United Kingdom

Lockdown the third, was into its twelfth week. This round presented a different challenge than the novelty of the first "stay at home" curfew. I had a message from the mother of my children. Our youngest son was in crisis. His psychotic, cannabis-induced episodes of eight years earlier had returned after spending three months bound to the house.

I pulled up outside the familiar house that had once been the place I call home. Unclipping the seatbelt, I rubbed my face breathing deeply, centering; at least trying to. A bus passed close to the wing mirror, brakes hissing down the steep hill beside the parked car. I recalled how we had, in that first winter after moving in, watched from the bedroom window as cars drove recklessly down that hill. Turning sidewards in the fresh snowfall, cars slid, crashing into others parked further down the slope. This year it was my son crashing. The ravaging demon of mental health unleashed once more, and after so much progress. Months of working from home isolation, separation from his friends, the false ignominy of living with his mother when others had traveled, studied, and worked in new places had tipped him over. I glanced to my right, through the car window, and where heart saw home, my head knew it no longer was; but a part of me, a portion of my history, still lived there. Not least the boy, now man, who was in pain again.

Closing the car door and crossing the road, I rang the doorbell. I noticed the edging of the lawn that I had put in place, the outside light that I had bought from a hotel that was shutting down. The door opened. My wife – no, ex-wife – looked both anxious and relieved. It was as though we were still together. Twenty-five years of shared life creates a bond, an ease of manner with the other that becomes automatic, especially in those seminal life moments where nothing need really be explained.

She stood to one side beckoning me in with her eyes. I wiped my feet on the matting overly long. The surge of emotion at seeing the familiarity of so many things still there unchanged welled up unbidden, threatening to overwhelm me for a moment. The door closed and she led on the back of the house and the kitchen. I passed the large driftwood assemblage still hanging on the hall wall. A memory of summer trips away together.

In the bright kitchen, I saw my pacing son and crossed to him. He stopped. He looked confused that this smaller, older man, was standing where he was about to walk. I stretched my arms to hold him. Our gap in age and size oddly contradictory. I was unsure that he would accept the hold, uncertain that it was the right thing to do, but instinct drove the act and I was both surprised and relieved at how long we stood there. My son's powerful arms rested with deceptive tenderness across my shoulders. I felt that I had, without words, said as much as I was capable of saying. Did he feel the same, I wondered?

We broke apart without looking directly at each other, and I turned to sit at the table whilst he resumed his restless pacing. The seconds turned to a minute. He paused beside his mother.

"It's okay, Dave. Dad wants to be here with you, too." She broke the silence.

Dave looked at her, bleached-blue eyes bigger than usual, unblinking, beseeching. He drew a meaty hand across his stubbled chin and resumed scratching hard at a reddened ear.

"Why're they doing this?"

"Sorry, what now love?"

"This! This fucking with my head! They've put something in my ear. It's here, I can feel it buzzing. It's hot. Feel it."

Our son, though full grown, remained a young, vulnerable adult. He sat at the table. His angst filled the kitchen — no, not the kitchen, the entire house — pulsing the very air. I could see my former wife's troubled face. Like me, striving to seem controlled, but internally I wept, frightened by the immense chasm of ignorance and impotence I felt in the face of his torment. He, demanding those who brought him into this world to give him the peace he craved, and we, self-loathing, filled with recrimination, questioning which part of our parenting had led to this.

He rose, towering over her, not just with height but sheer volume. He increasingly resembled a young Henry VIII, as the anti-psychotic stealthily added weight to his frame. He leaned his head, muscular neck tensed, inviting her to touch his ear. It had scratch marks from where he repeatedly fiddled and pulled at it.

He fixed his mother with pale dull eyes.

"When did they put it there? I had an ear infection. Year 3, was it Year 3?"

He needed her to tell him. To acknowledge and confirm that they are controlling him and reading his thoughts as he says they are.

"That's a long time ago son. I don't think anyone —"

"Oh, so you think I'm crazy, eh? Are you part it too? You're the one letting them access the house!" His head jutted in challenge and she shifted sideways away from the table a little.

"Now, no one is saying you're crazy," I interjected, exchanging glances with my ex-wife, reunited in our concern. "Everyone has had too much time alone. We all have those accusing voices from time to time. It's just got louder for you. You haven't stopped taking your aripiprazole have —"

"For fuck's sake! It's nothing to do with that shit. They are part of the conspiracy. Why are they saying these things? The voices are chatting shit about me. It's got nothing to do with the fucking drugs. I don't want them to give me more shit just to make me fucking dopey!" His fist punctuated his rant, banging the table rhythmically through his final sentence. Glasses jiggled in the wall cupboard. I lowered my eyes and sipped at my cold coffee.

"What do they stand to gain, eh? Why are they saying these things? Like the birds are chatting stuff at me too. It's fucking doing my head in. Why can't it just stop?"

"Dave's unplugged all his electronic devices. Haven't you love? That's how they started talking to him. Through the technology."

"But Dave," I said, "this is coming from inside, your inner voice, not outside. It's because —"

"Right, so you're saying you don't believe what I'm telling you either?" Dave stood, his voice getting louder, slower, more insistent. "Why can't you just understand. I just want them to stop."

"Okay, I'm sorry. It's real for you."

"Course it's real. You think I'm —"

"No. I see it's real. So, what exactly are…they saying?"

"They say loads of stuff. They're trying to humiliate me. Like, last night. Budge and Tom were telling me to jump under a train. Laughing at me and shit. And Russ was sitting there, like psychoanalyzing the shit out of me and saying I'm fucking crazy. I don't like it. When I go to bed, they read my thoughts while I'm asleep."

His mother stood at the sink, staring out to the garden, as our son's thoughts poured out. I stared at her back. The strain of worry, years of care showing in the slump of her shoulders. She continued to face the window. I looked away from the woman who had carried and borne my son. The guilt-ridden consciousness that perhaps my departure from them a decade ago had likely precipitated this very moment, completely drained my authority to know anything about anything.

"Come on son, why would old school friends be saying that? You haven't seen them in ages. If they knew you were distressed like this, they'd be really —"

"Yeah, so why are they joining in, eh? I don't know why. And the fucking birds?"

From the sink, without turning back into the room, his mother spoke.

"Dave woke me this morning at four-thirty." She paused, gathering herself. "I heard him in the bathroom retching. When I went in, he had his fingers down his throat, kneeling by the lavatory."

"I was trying to get them out! They've…like…put microchips in my throat. And my ear. I need to get a scan…today. Ring the surgery."

"We can't until eight o'clock, son."

"You're not taking it seriously, are you though? Like why they're chatting shit at me…I just want it to stop. I've got a scar on the back of my head."

Dave spoke in spasmodic bursts between which he seemed absent, elsewhere. He paced the squareness of the room, shuffling slowly, without purpose, back and forth. Lifting to sit on the worktop, shifting to a chair, passing the stove, hitting the gas knobs with the side of a clenched fist. They click and spark – dot, dot dash, a coded message that we could hear but not understand.

"That's where they slipped the chip into my head. They monitor what I'm thinking. Like they know what I'm thinking. It's bloody freaky. I need a scan…find it. Cut it out."

Circling to the table he collected up a pouch of tobacco, papers, and lighter. He has the dazed hesitancy of a sleepwalker, the overly careful movement of the very drunk trying to look sober. Frowning under gathered brows, a bright-eyed stare of hurt reproach at each of us in turn, he opened the door to the garden, and exited to smoke.

"I've called Pete," she said, "visits from his brother usually help temper the episodes."

"Thank you," I raised my eyes to hers. "For all you've done. And still do."

She looked uncomfortable. We sat in awkward silence.

"What has the mental health team suggested?" I asked.

"It's hard to tell. I try to overhear, but only hear what Dave says."

"Has he been taking his medication?"

"As far as I can tell. Definitely these last few days because I've seen him do it."

"They'll increase the dose, I guess. Is Pete coming over?"

She nodded.

"Pete will be here soon. He's better when he sees other people. You should come more." She rushed out the final sentence as the backdoor opened. Her head turned to meet Dave with a weak smile. He entered along with the odor of cigarettes.

"What?" he barked, glaring a challenge at us.

He knew our silence was recent.

"You think I'm crazy. Those birds they're chatting about me now, out there, just now, like you two, in here." His arms waved to indicate the places to which he referred. He dropped the roll up paraphernalia on the bleached pine table with a sigh and renewed his circuits of the kitchen.

The silence lasted a little too long. I stood and intercepted my son's perambulation. We embraced again and I spoke into his shoulder.

"When your key worker calls, can you give her permission to talk to either mum or I?"

I asked, unsure what the response will be, and the meekness of his reply undoes me. This powerfully built young man, almost relieved, assured us that he would allow the care team to talk to us. He became a small boy, half his size, wanting us, his parents, to make the world right again. I shook as a sob rose and convulsed my body once, twice, before regaining control.

Three weeks passed as the increased dose of aripiprazole first knocked Dave out, and then returned him to us, calmer and less questioning. Each of us played our part in the support program. His brother and I paid open-door visits to the home gym, cheering him on and serving as personal trainers. His mother encouraged his artistic endeavors, buying fresh canvases and tubes of paint, and slowly, but surely, the voices subsided, and our family regrouped.

The Immutability of Life

Edwina Toulmin

40, New South Wales, Australia

Forty was meant to look like a slender woman in a four-wheel-drive BMW, lugging children and sports gear between private school and a renovated Californian bungalow; big rock on her hand signaling the possession of a doctor or lawyer to pay for it all.

From an early age I had mapped out the bearing of my future: finish school and go to university, graduate at twenty-two, get married at twenty-four, have two children (a girl and a boy), and live happily ever after. And for many years, I appeared on track to achieve what I'd set out to. I was not a brilliant student, but I worked hard and achieved high marks, obtaining a place in Medical Science at Sydney University. I met Carlos in my first week there. Charismatic and funny, but also gentlemanly and sweet, Carlos seemed unable to go anywhere on campus without his retinue of admiring girls. Somehow, I stood out among the others and he asked me out. I said yes immediately. Ours was a fun relationship, and we laughed a lot. We developed a vast repertoire of inside jokes and phrases that mystified our friends, but amused us greatly.

We agreed to put off marriage until we'd both completed our studies in science and dentistry, with Carlos proposing on our tenth anniversary. The wedding was held two years later. After twelve years in the making, it was perfect – not a detail overlooked. The ceremony was held in the Great Hall of Sydney University, our wedding photos taken on the campus where we'd met so many years before.

Life settled down. The dream wedding was over, the presents opened and the thank you cards sent. Our careers were starting out nicely, and we were both earning well. We began looking for a house to buy and talked about starting a family. Life, however, is a cunning trickster, and has a way of lulling you into a false sense of ease before jerking you quickly back out of it. It was only a few months after the wedding that I learned of Carlos's secret life, a life conducted in the public toilets of shopping centers and the beds of strange men.

I thought it would take about six months to recover from the divorce, so when I'm still in pain after two years, crying most nights and consoling myself on the weekends with pinot noir and boxes of pizza, I take myself off to a psychologist. I think I am there to talk about my ex-husband, so I'm confused when she spends most of the session asking about my family life. She draws two stick figures on the whiteboard, one standing upright and one leaning on the other. Then she rubs out the upright figure, which she has named Carlos, and points to the now keeling-over figure she has given my name. I understand the narrative, but do not quite know how it applies to me.

Adrift. That is what life can feel like at times. Like you are a flimsy piece of seaweed, tossed around on the seas of life. But if I am the seaweed, Mark is the sand. The substrate into which I can develop firm roots and flourish.

I meet him at a farewell party for his brother. He makes me laugh so hard I have tears slashing mascara-stained tracks through my foundation. We are soon on the dance floor, shouting lyrics to eighties pop songs into each other's ears until the club closes and everyone piles out onto the street and into a pie shop. He makes a sweet speech about how nice it was to have met me, but that unfortunately he is returning to England in a few days so won't have a chance to get to know me more. I suggest to him that perhaps we could steal a few more hours together, call a taxi, and take him back to my place.

It is only when I am driving away after breakfast with Mark and his family the next day that I realize what I have done. I have begun to fall for this man, another one who flits out of my grasp whenever I clutch at him, only for a different reason this time.

It begins with a farewell text, and then another when he has landed safely back in the UK. A message every few days soon becomes a daily message. Then twice daily. Then a phone call. Before long, we are talking two or three times a day, often for hours at a time. What is there to talk about for all those hours everyone wants to know. "Everything" is the answer. He is patient and understanding when my anxiety blazes. He runs a martial arts school in his spare time, sings in a band, and knows how to renovate a house. His Yorkshire accent at once amuses and befuddles me, with phrases such as "mouth like a blown-out fuse box" and "as mad as a box of frogs" causing me endless entertainment. I visit him in Leeds, he visits me again in Sydney.

We realize it is serious and decide we must be together. My business can't run itself, and I can't afford to pay someone to run it for me, so we agree he must come to Australia. At forty-three, he is unable to simply step on a plane, holiday visa flapping in hand. His job is not on the skills shortages list, so that is not an option either. We devise a plan to get him over here on a holiday visa, which we think we will swap for a partner visa after he's lived with me for a year and we can claim de facto status.

Small issue: He is already married. Separated, but married. He can't come out until the divorce is finalized.

With every month, there is another delay in the divorce proceedings. I tell him I'll give him a year, that I didn't sign up for a pen pal. A year passes, and no divorce. He asks me to give him more time. My friends tell me to give him more time. Eventually, we realize that he doesn't need to be divorced to be eligible for the partner visa; he can come to Australia before the divorce is finalized. We are ecstatic. He quits his job and begins to work through his three-month notice period.

But suddenly people start wearing masks in the street, and my supplies at work are getting low. A virus has been circulating in China, but this barely registers with us. Surely it will be like bird flu, like Ebola? A developing world problem. Except now the virus has spread to Italy and there is footage on the news of Italians rallying each other with song. People in China are dropping like flies in hospital corridors. The virus is in England, too. The Australian border closes. We tell ourselves that it will be over in six months.

There is a purple lump on my side, just below my belly button. It appeared during the divorce, and I showed it to the doctor who said it was nothing to worry about. Lately, the lump has been getting larger. It is itchy and sore. I ask the GP for a referral to a dermatologist, who also says it is nothing. I insist on having it removed because it is ugly. "If you insist," she huffs, and sends me off for an ultrasound. This is the year that I turn forty, and as the radiographer spreads the cold gloop over my tummy, I can't help but think of all my friends, every one of them now, who has lain on a similar couch to have this same gloop spread over their pregnant bellies. All I have managed to grow is a lump. As I notice the edges of my eyes glisten with this knowledge, the radiographer clears her throat. "Um, I'll just...I don't think it's anything... but I'll just...go and get the doctor."

She is away for ten minutes, so I have plenty of time to observe the long, white, tree-like structure pictured in the scan that has its leaves in my skin and its roots tickling my abdominal wall. It looks – well, cancerous. I am trying to calm myself with breathing exercises when the radiographer returns and dismisses me wordlessly. "See? Nothing to worry about," I console myself.

You never want a doctor to call you out of hours. The dermatologist rings just after eight on a Monday morning and tells me I have a rare form of skin cancer. She tells me the name, but it is a blur of words and I miss it, too stunned to ask her to repeat it. Can I come in this afternoon to talk more? I manage to arrange the appointment, writing the time down so I don't forget. I am worried I will forget, because my brain has started doing backflips in its shell and I don't think it can process numbers anymore.

We apply for a travel exemption so Mark can come to Australia to be with me for the cancer treatment, but it is rejected within days. He tries his best to comfort me over the phone. When I complain that the surgery has now pulled my belly button to one side, he christens it the Picasso Belly Button, making said belly button bounce up and down with laughter. I say I don't like the scar and he says not to worry, that scars are cool. He jokes that it looks like a cartoon scar and he is right: there is a wide horizontal slash from one hip to the other, criss-crossed at intervals by vertical pink lines. It looks as though someone has drawn it on in pink Texta.

The dermatologist is pleased with her work. "It just looks like a really big c-section scar," she reassures me. But it is not that, I think. I have the scar, but nothing to show for it. No happy family in a world that seems full of happy, oblivious families.

It is all too much. I have waited a lifetime for my Happily Ever After, and a year and a half to be with this man. Now, just as I think the dream is within my grasp, our plans are blown out of our hands and into the hands of Australian Immigration.

It isn't until July that I snap. We are on a Facetime call so I can see him stop dead in the middle of his kitchen when I tell him it is all too hopeless, that I think we should end it. He begs me to reconsider, but after a month of thinking about it and talking it over, my heart has solidified, and I am more resolved than ever. He tells me that this is a protective mechanism, that I am trying to protect myself from being hurt. I agree with him, but I am powerless to stop it. There is a growth like the growth in my abdomen that has crept around my heart and cut off the blood supply. It goes black with necrosis and cannot respond to his gentle love now.

I tell myself I didn't really want all that happy family stuff, anyway. Tell myself that men are too much trouble and children are a pain. I flip between swearing off men for life and flicking desperately through Tinder, rarely daring to go on a date but reassuring myself that if I wanted to, there were plenty of men to choose from. I return to past boyfriends. I attempt to distract myself by spoiling myself with expensive fortieth birthday presents. I fall in love with a pair of Gucci espadrilles and pay fifteen hundred dollars for them. I buy thousands of dollars' worth of art and plaster my apartment walls with it. I finally get around to pulling apart my engagement and wedding rings, converting them into a necklace, with Argyle pink diamonds interspersing the diamonds from Carlos. Anything, anything, to make that pain go away.

Mark does not give up. He sends flowers, chocolate, wine, and cards. He asks to speak to me on the phone so he can wish me a happy Christmas, but only if I'm okay with it. I think about it for a few days before I reluctantly agree. We talk for four and a half hours and it is as if the last six months of the Great Freeze had never happened. I know immediately that it doesn't matter if I never see him in person again: he is the One.

We resolve to work to be together, somehow. We speak to an immigration lawyer and craft a complicated plan involving travel exemptions, tourist visas, and multiple pieces of evidence of a continuing and committed relationship. Each day is split between frantic searching for a solution that will reunite us and a crippling inability to achieve even the smallest of goals as the hopelessness of the situation presses heavily on my mind.

The lawyer tells us she will submit an application for Mark to travel to Australia if we wish, but that it is highly unlikely it will be successful. She flippantly suggests I spend six to twelve months in the UK instead. "But I have a business to run," I say. She is silent.

I think about it for a while. I can use the money I've been saving for a second property to live off while I'm over there. I needed a break from work, anyway. We tell our lawyer we'd like to submit a travel exemption for me to go to the UK under the new category of travel for three or more months. She has us both write a statutory declaration stating that I will be living with Mark while I am over there, has me provide proof of the money I will live off of, and asks for a statement from my therapist about the impact of our separation on my mental health. We do all this, and it is rejected immediately. We resubmit and, finally, it is approved.

In six weeks, it is all organized. I have found a dentist to keep the practice going, Mum and Dad are looking after my dog, I pack my bag and get on a plane. Mark picks me up from the airport and drives me to his place, a small and dilapidated row house – he is not a rich man. I quickly get used to my humble lodgings, and within days, all the stress and anxiety I have been suffering starts slipping away.

We spend most of our time exploring the countryside, walking through woods and over moorland, up hills and along little streams. He loves showing me the vibrant, green fecundity of an English summer and the birds and animals that seem to have jumped straight out of a children's storybook and into the scenes before us.

Those magic three months are over now – my business has suffered enough and I am running out of money. While I was there, we submitted three more applications with Australian Immigration for him to travel back to Australia with me, and each one was rejected within days. The lawyers tell us we need more evidence of commitment: shared bank accounts, a registered relationship, engagement, or even marriage. His divorce is still at least three months away from being finalized and we are afraid of doing any of those things lest it complicates the divorce proceedings. The Australian Prime Minister is promising to keep the borders closed for another year, at least. I will be nearing forty-two by then, the final few days of my fertility quickly ticking by. For now, I am stuck in Fortress Australia and Mark is stuck in England. Who knows when we will be together again.

For now, forty looks like a middle-aged woman who ferries her dog between the New York loft-style apartment and private dental clinic she owns. A woman who wears the rock around her neck, not on her finger. A woman who doesn't need a doctor to bankroll her life because she can pay for it herself. A woman who gave up on the love of her life because COVID made him impossible, and then accepted impossible. A woman who is making the best of the life she has, not the life she planned. The lesson of my forties: the immutability of life.

Senior Math

Carlton Clayton
62, North Carolina, United States

I was cooped up in a house with a child whose arithmetic attention span was shorter than a three-inch ruler and with third-grade math problems I couldn't solve. I cussed COVID-19, the teachers, the school, the school district, the administration, pencils, the computer, the governor, bikes, my incoming texts' ringtone, trains, airplanes, the tower of London, and math books. Especially math books. It was personal.

It was August, the beginning of the 2020-2021 school year, and my daughter was entering third grade. During the summer I had to choose whether to have her attend school in person or be assigned to fully remote learning. I have the trifecta of the coronavirus vulnerabilities: black, male, and over sixty-years-old. Though it is proven that children are less susceptible to the virus, I didn't want to take any chances, so I chose fully remote learning as I didn't want her to potentially catch the virus at school and bring it home to me.

Thinking an actual school desk would put her in the classroom mindset, I bought her a combination desk and chair with a book rack beneath the chair and a groove for pencils at the front of the desk. My desk and computer were opposite hers, so I was facing away.

It was difficult keeping her on point, especially with the math. I had to listen in and follow her classes in order to keep up with her assignments, particularly the homework. At the end of class, she never knew what the homework was even though the teacher had repeated it several times. I'd ask her and she would shrug her shoulders: "I don't know." Occasionally, I would look over my shoulder at her when she'd gone quiet. She'd be staring blankly at the screen, sucking on the two middle fingers of her right hand and twirling her hair with her left.

Science, reading, language arts, and social studies were unproblematic. But third grade math was not as simple as I expected it to be. Math is taught differently now than it was when I sat in a classroom at James City Elementary School. It's like the distributive property on steroids. There is mental math and models, place-value blocks, open number lines, and arrays.

In order to add 20+55, first one has to draw a horizontal line then add vertical hash marks along the line specifically marking every fifth and tenth place. The number 20 is placed at the far left of the line and to get the sum of the two numbers, bowed lines are drawn (like bunny hops), connecting every tenth hashmark until it reaches 75. (The subtraction using this method is beyond my means of explanation.) And there is the array. To multiply 9x5, one has to make an array of five circles or squares in rows and columns, five across and nine down, then add them. It took ten minutes for her to do that with me coaching. I had to sit and wait for her to draw those circles, one by one. Then came the big one: trying to explain the difference between 9x5 and 5x9. It was like explaining the difference between a road and a street. They both get you there. Multiplying 9x5 is 5, nine times, while 5x9 is 9, five times. That makes sense to a sixty-two-year-old, but it wasn't me I was teaching.

In the middle of that lesson my daughter leaned across her desk with an outstretched arm, the pencil loosely tethered to her fingers, and rested a side of her face on her upper arm. I knew it was over, but I tried to salvage it. "Sit up, girl, and pay attention," I said. She rolled her eyes at me and let out a long, disgruntled sigh as if it were too great an effort to raise her torso and sit back in the chair.

"Lord help me Jesus," I whispered half comically.

"Why does He need to help you? I'm the one who has to do this stuff."

I couldn't let her see the smile spreading across my face. "I gotta go to the bathroom," I announced, avoiding eye contact with her. "Do your work," I commanded, "and don't you move. Don't...move!"

When I returned she was spinning on the tile like a ballerina, the whipped air ballooning her dress. She likes wearing dresses for that purpose. It was 11:23, and class ended at 11:30. I let her spin.

One morning, the students were instructed to go to a certain website. Everyone was having difficulty getting in. The teacher spelled out the site several times and continued explaining the procedure, but no one could access it. I tried multiple times on my computer without success. It was close to mayhem as some of the parents expressed their frustrations. After about fifteen minutes the teacher flashed the correct website address on the screen. It was a totally different site from the one she had been providing.

She just put it out there without explanation, apology, or remorse and continued talking as though it had been the correct address all along. I blew my top.

"This is fucking bullshit," I said. My hands came down hard upon her desk, the pencil sailed through the air. "Just goddamned bullshit."

She looked at me with worried surprise. "You said the F-word, Daddy."

"I'm sorry, sweetie," I said, brushing back her hair. "I'm sorry — fucking bullshit! A goddamned waste of time." She looked at me with anxious eyes. I didn't apologize that time because I had another "bullshit" lying in wait.

I stood in front of her tablet in full view of her teacher, and with a steady finger I clicked out of the session. "Get your shoes on, sweetie, we're going to the park," I said. Clicking out of the session abruptly was my version of storming out of class and slamming the door behind me — my senior moment. I put her bike in the car, and we set off to Freedom Park in Charlotte's Dillworth section.

We circled the pond several times, she on the bike and I close by, making every effort to prevent her from plunging into the green, murky water. It was a hot day out, and there were no clouds to abate the sun's breath. I was anxious to settle on a bench under a tree near the amphitheater. She laid her bike down and went over to explore. A young couple sat on a nearby bench cuddled close, the husband rolling a bassinet stroller back and forth with an outstretched arm.

Slumped on the bench, I spread my arms along the back rest, my fingers dancing to a silent tune. I couldn't get the math session out of my head. It was all I could think about. I wrestled with it and let it drag me under like a fisherman's cast net, thinking about the open number lines, arrays, open-ended circles, and lopsided squares. "Fucking bullshit," I muttered. The couple unlocked their embrace and looked over. I looked away.

My daughter returned and sat next to me, kicking her legs out. She leaned into me. I met her eyes. "You okay now, Daddy?"

I was sorry for letting her see me like that, and it was hard to look directly at her now.

"Yes, I'm okay," I said.

The other reason I had chosen remote learning for my daughter was that I wanted to test my teaching skills. Being a teacher had been a lifelong dream ever since I sat in my fifth grade classroom at James City Elementary School. This was my golden opportunity. But the challenges of new math and an uninterested child proved daunting tasks, and I wasn't succeeding.

After that day, I decided to teach my daughter math the way I learned it – the way she's going to use it in real life. I taught her how to multiply and add numbers horizontally and vertically and how to carry over in addition and to borrow in subtraction. She learned the order of adding and multiplying numbers set off parenthetically. And she learned that 5x9 and 9x5 get to the same place, but one takes a street and the other takes a road.

A few months later, school returned to in-person format, and I had the option of keeping my daughter fully remote or sending her to class. As much as I worried about contracting COVID-19, I thought long and hard about taking the risk just to get away from the math. But I decided to stay the course.

It took a lot of whining, grunting, foot stomping, manic sighs, verbal outbursts, and door slamming – all on my part – but we got through it. She got a 97 in math for the first quarter, and she ended up receiving awards for math excellence and reading achievement. She even received an award for character.

I couldn't teach the new math because I refused to accept it, but I discovered that it wasn't just the math, it was me. I was too stubborn to learn it, even for the sake of my daughter. I stepped back and let her figure it out on her own. I continued to listen in and monitor her participation, but I left her learning up to her. As she said, she had to do the work. And I had to let her do it.

Fifty years ago we had far fewer distractions, so our attention was more focused. There were only three channels on TV, no Nintendo or YouTube or iPhone or personal computers or wireless music or virtual realities. The way I learned fifty years ago is perhaps not the best method for today's children. Today, learning has to be imparted in any scheme that profits the learner, even if it involves traveling around the Milky Way just to get to the moon.

I recently received an email from the school about the possibility of remote learning for the upcoming school year, and they wanted the parents' input. At least I think that's what it said. Once I saw the words remote, upcoming, and school I deleted the email. My daughter will be in a live classroom next year. I'd rather deal with a bout of COVID-19 than have to face virtual fourth-grade math.

Listening to Kendi

Elizabeth Kleinfeld
51, Colorado, United States

"Do you want to listen to the Kendi book?"

That was the question I asked my husband, Tom, every night at 5 p.m. I had an alarm set on my phone to remind me to ask it because although I asked it every night, our days had become so scrambled that the only way I could reliably do anything was to have an external reminder. My phone rattled all day, reminding me to give Tom his drugs (14 different drugs, three times a day), get him up and dressed, get myself dressed, walk the dogs, check his surgical wound for infection, give him breakfast, give myself breakfast, and so on. In between reacting to alarms, I taught my classes remotely and mediocrely, grateful that the pandemic had forced me to work from home because it allowed me to be my husband's around-the-clock caregiver.

The Kendi book was Ibram X. Kendi's *How To Be an Antiracist*, the 2019 book that became a 2020 must-read when the Black Lives Matter movement began grabbing headlines, and white people started wondering if being nice was enough. We learned it wasn't.

Three months into the 2020 COVID lockdown, Tom — healthy and fit at 61 — came home from a road trip to Oregon, where he had hiked and rode motorcycles with his brother, sat on the porch with me with a mojito in hand, and had a massive stroke that rendered him paralyzed on his left side, with significant cognitive challenges and a condition called left neglect that made him unaware of anything that happened on his left. He spent most of the summer in the hospital, first in the neurological ICU, then the regular neuro unit, and finally graduated to the rehab wing of the hospital before coming home in late July.

Physical, occupational, and speech therapists came to the house Monday through Friday, masked and with hand sanitizer. A couple times a week, we went to appointments with neurologists, pain specialists, and other doctors, where we sat socially distanced in waiting rooms before finally being allowed a few minutes with a doctor who inevitably told Tom something he didn't want to hear: he was unlikely to walk again, the pain treatment he was curious about probably wouldn't work for him, the perpetual headache might never go away.

Between appointments, Tom napped and sharpened knives, the hobby he had picked up to replace tinkering with motorcycles, while I taught and attended meetings via Zoom. By evening, we were both spent and Tom often suggested he go to bed rather than eat dinner. I always insisted he at least come to the table and try some dinner, which was a quiet affair. He had to concentrate on chewing and swallowing to keep from choking on his food because the stroke had rendered his brain unable to coordinate the movements of his throat muscles, so we weren't able to have conversations. After a couple weeks of this awkward arrangement, I suggested we listen to an audiobook during dinner to fill the silence.

I had seen references to the Kendi book and watched a few video clips of him speaking. Tom and I had been talking about the Black Lives Matter movement, and his son and I had both participated in protests. Tom said he wanted to learn more about it, so we easily agreed that we'd start our audiobook habit with *How To Be an Antiracist*.

Tom's speech therapist had been working with him on cognition and memory and encouraged him to integrate techniques such as summarizing and paraphrasing what he heard or read into daily activities. As we listened to Kendi narrate his book each night, I did my best to weave the summarizing and paraphrasing exercises in.

Tom wanted to hear each chapter twice to make sure, as he put it, his "stroke-scrambled brain got it," so we listened to a chapter at dinner and then listened to the same chapter again after I had gotten him into bed. After his stroke, I had moved our bed up from the basement to the living room, where it hid behind a curtain. Every night, I undressed Tom, changed his urinary bag, stretched his paralyzed left leg and arm to keep the muscles from stiffening and shortening, massaged pain cream into both legs and his left arm, gave him medications for nerve pain, heart arrhythmia, blood pressure, anxiety, depression, headache, dementia, and generalized pain, and got his legs and left arm arranged to avoid pressure sores, often propping pillows under them or tipping Tom partially onto one side and squeezing rolled up towels or foam wedges between his body and the mattress. The process exhausted both of us.

With Tom in bed and me sitting on the floor next to the bed, we listened to each chapter a second time. He sometimes drifted off and I had to wake him up. After the chapter finished playing, I prompted him to summarize it. On a good night, he haltingly repeated the gist of the chapter, sometimes adding a disclaimer like "I didn't really follow what he said about why policy is important." Other nights he would say, "Sorry, babe, I couldn't track what he was saying this time." On those nights, I summarized for him, hoping he would interrupt at some point to finish the summary, but he was usually asleep before I got three sentences out.

Each night before beginning a new chapter, I asked him if he wanted to review the previous chapter, prompting him to summarize what he remembered. One night when he didn't recall much, I said, "Remember, the last chapter was about –" but before I could finish my sentence, Tom angrily cut me off.

"No, I don't remember! I had a stroke, *remember*?" The second remember was emphasized ironically. I stopped talking and started the audiobook.

Some evenings after he finished eating, we talked about the ideas in the chapter, moving beyond the speech therapist's summarizing and paraphrasing exercises. Other nights, conversation was more difficult. One night, I asked Tom what was most interesting to him about the chapter we had just listened to. He was silent. I had learned to give him plenty of time to respond to questions, but I wondered, was he pondering my question? Processing the reading? Falling asleep?

Just as I was about to put my hand on his shoulder to get his attention, he said, "Remind me why 'not racist' doesn't work."

"Kendi says the opposite of racist is antiracist," I explained. "'Not racist' tries to invent a neutral ground between the two, but because it doesn't challenge racism it isn't antiracist."

He nodded slowly. "I tried to explain that to my mom, but I got confused."

I asked him if he wanted to paraphrase it back to me so it would be easier to explain to his mom. "I want to go to bed," he said, his head hanging heavily. He'd had both physical and occupational therapy that day.

One day in mid-October Tom announced he wanted to sit in on the class I was teaching on being a writing tutor. Because I was teaching remotely, sitting in simply meant getting him set up at his laptop and logging him into the online platform my class used for meetings. During class, a student asked me how to help a tutee who got an F on a paper because they used what their professor considered to be nonstandard English.

"Let's talk about grading policies that rely on the concepts of standard and nonstandard English," I responded. "Whose English is considered standard and whose English is considered nonstandard?" In the ensuing class discussion, students determined that the English of white people is considered standard and the English of Black people is considered nonstandard.

"Is the problem in the people speaking these different Englishes or in the policy that deems one English better than another?" I asked.

After class, I checked on Tom at his laptop in the living room. He got a serious look on his face and took my hand.

"Babe, I think you're an antiracist. That makes me proud." He fell silent but kept holding my hand. I wanted to remind him that Kendi says being an antiracist isn't a permanent state, but fluid based on what actions someone is taking at any particular moment. I was not comfortable claiming the status of antiracist after one good class. But before I could formulate what I wanted to say, Tom spoke again.

"Can I take a nap?"

A few nights later, after listening to a chapter during dinner, instead of asking to go to bed, Tom said, "I want to listen to that one again and take notes." I got his journal and started the chapter up, curious about what he was writing the one time he did put pen to paper. He was too tired for conversation when the chapter ended. After I got him to bed, I looked at what he had written in his journal: "dog fight, Woody vs. Luna, no winner." I hadn't noticed the dogs fighting while we listened to the chapter. Had something in the Kendi chapter reminded him of the dogs fighting? When I asked him about it the next morning, he laughed. "I don't know what that was about, babe," he said.

Later that month, the home healthcare agency that provided the physical, occupational, and speech therapists called. Because of COVID, they were having staffing shortages and wouldn't be able to send anyone out for at least a week. Tom happened to not have any doctor's appointments for a week, so with Denver on lockdown and it being too cold out to visit with his mom or our adult children on the porch, Tom and I spent a week at home, just the two of us and Kendi. Without the distractions of therapy, appointments, or visitors, we were able to finish the book, even listening again to some of the earlier chapters that Tom said he had forgotten and wanted to review.

When a new occupational therapist showed up, the first person we'd seen in the flesh in nearly two weeks, she complimented Tom on his mask, which looked like the recently deceased Supreme Court Justice Ruth Bader Ginsburg's dissent collar. "Thanks," he said. "I love RBG. And I'm learning how to be antiracist."

She looked surprised. "I've heard of a racist," she said, "but what's an antiracist?"

He looked over at me and nodded, as if to say, *I've got this, babe. Watch.*

"It's from this book we've been listening to," he said and turned to me. "What's the guy's name?"

"Ibram X. Kendi," I said.

"Right, Kendi. He says the opposite of racist isn't 'not racist,' it's antiracist. There's no such thing as 'not racist.' You either support racism or you work against it," he said. "To be antiracist you've got to actively challenge racism."

As Tom and the OT talked, first about antiracism and then about the limitations brought on by his stroke, I thought about how a year ago, we were rafting on the Colorado River, just us and two friends. Tom's body and mind were strong as he rowed us past autumn foliage and rugged shoreline. He would never be on the river again.

After his OT session, Tom asked me to push him in his wheelchair over to the window.

"Good job explaining antiracism to the OT," I said.

"Thanks, babe," he said.

We looked out at the trees losing their leaves.

Part IV: Fall

Unblinded

Heather C. Morris
38, Alabama, United States

In August 2020, only five months into a brutal global pandemic, pharmaceutical companies around the world were careening headlong toward the world's great hope — a safe and effective vaccine for COVID-19. But the frontrunners, the Pfizer and Moderna mRNA vaccines, were new technologies. To many people, these companies appeared to be flying blind.

My phone buzzed. I glanced at the unknown ten-digit number. Should I answer? Probably one of those warranty expiration calls.

I answered.

"Hello?" My voice was hesitant, my thumb poised to punch the red button if a human did not immediately respond.

"Hello, is this Mrs. Heather Morris?"

Ah! A human!

"Yes, this is she."

"I'm calling from the Medical Affiliated Research Center here in town. It appears that you filled out a form to be considered for the upcoming Phase 3 Pfizer vaccine trial. Would you be available to answer a few questions? It may take about thirty minutes."

A brisk breeze lifted my hair, bringing with it the summer scent of grass. A lawn mower rumbled in a nearby yard as the sun emerged from behind a cloud. I felt like I could see more clearly.

Five minutes ago, I was consumed with all the questions a person must ask post-COVID: how long should I stay at a public pool, even outdoors and highly spaced? Were our kids ever going to return to in-person learning? What is the exact definition of exposure? While our community never imposed as many stringent lockdown restrictions as larger metropolitan areas, our everyday existence was far from normal. As evidenced by this abnormal phone call.

An abnormality which also offered a glimpse of hope.

A few weeks before, an advertisement had popped up on my Instagram feed:

Interested in participating in a vaccine trial? Clinical trials taking applications in your area.

CLICK HERE

I clicked.

"Hey, Chris," I turned to my husband, lounging on his side of the bed. "I'd like to apply to be in a COVID vaccine trial. And…

I just thought…like I should make sure you were good with it first. Like, just in case something happened…which it won't," I trailed off.

He had given me a long look, "Sure. Sounds like something you would want to do."

"Okay, then. Great."

A few questions later, I had pressed "submit." I felt like I had entered some perverse lottery.

Had I wanted to win? Oddly…YES!

And a few weeks later, lounging poolside, I got "the call," and I knew deep down that I desperately wanted to be accepted into this trial. More than I had wanted anything in a long time.

My background and training is in molecular microbiology. I spent years and years in laboratory after laboratory, devising ways to "see" molecules that were far too small to see, even with a microscope. After spending all that time in research labs, I became comfortable with the unknown and with the process of science.

And now I was given an opportunity to be involved in one of the biggest scientific achievements of my time.

On the phone with the clinician, I answered question after question. I sailed through the first few.

"Have you ever participated in a clinical trial before?"

"No."

"Are you willing to commit to multiple in-person appointments, including bloodwork?"

"Yes."

"Are you able to put yourself in positions or places where you could possibly be exposed to the coronavirus? Or do you completely isolate?"

This is it, I thought, the part where I tell them that I am the designated shopper in the family, that we attend church in masks, that my kids will be attending in-person learning as soon as they can...and this guy will say, "Thanks, but no thanks."

I listed off everything above to the clinician.

"Good," he said, "we are looking for trial participants who could possibly be exposed to the virus in order to test vaccine efficacy."

I was absurdly happy. It was only later that I pondered the oddity of his statement – trial participants must be people willing to put themselves in harm's way with no assurance of protection.

We scheduled my first appointment, I verified the directions to the research center and hung up. I immediately called Chris.

"They just called! I'm in!"

"Huh? Who called? In what?"

"Remember? I signed up for the Phase 3 COVID vaccine trial? Turns out Pfizer is the one conducting trials here in our city and they called and I'm in." I was grinning. Why was I grinning?

And with his response, I knew once again why I married this man, "That's awesome! I am so proud of you."

My first appointment was paperwork, bloodwork, more questions, signatures, and finally, an injection.

My nurse reminded me immediately before jabbing the needle into my upper arm, "Remember, this is a double-blind trial.

I have no idea – no one in this office has any idea – whether you are receiving the vaccine or the placebo."

"Right," I nodded and crossed my fingers, hoping for some pain around the injection site, which might mean I had gotten the vaccine.

Three weeks later, I was back in the office for an exact repeat – the second dose. As part of the trial, I was required to fill out a weekly COVID journal using a specific app downloaded to my phone. Every week, I was asked one question:

Have you experienced any of the following:

- o   A diagnosis of COVID-19
- o   Fever
- o   New or increased cough
- o   New or increased shortness of breath
- o   Chills
- o   New or increased muscle pain
- o   New loss of taste or smell
- o   Sore throat
- o   Diarrhea
- o   Vomiting

_____Yes _____ No

Months passed. Cases soared as winter approached. I continued to fill out my diary, always selecting No.

Our family was tested for COVID multiple times, always negative. My parents contracted COVID; friends lost their sense of taste and smell. I wondered if perhaps I had gotten the vaccine,

131

not the placebo. How else could I be avoiding this pervasive virus? It was everywhere I looked.

The very ubiquity of COVID cases allowed the trials to proceed faster. Because more trial participants were exposed to COVID, clear patterns emerged in the collected data – both Moderna and Pfizer vaccines were 95% effective in preventing infection. By December, both companies began to "unblind" their trial participants. Late that month, my phone vibrated.

"Is this Mrs. Heather Morris?"

"Yes."

"Hello Mrs. Morris. We are calling because we are unblinding subsets of our participants. Are you over the age of 65?"

"No."

"Ok. Sorry, you will have to wait." We both hung up.

A few weeks later, the familiar phone number appeared on my home screen.

"Is this Mrs. Heather Morris?"

"Yep."

"Hello Mrs. Morris, we are calling because we are unblinding subsets of our participants. Are you either a frontline worker or do you have a pre-existing, underlying condition?"

"No. Not a frontline worker and no underlying conditions."

"Ok. Thank you. You will have to wait."

As a healthy, 30-something, I was pretty sure I would be one of the last to know my vaccination status. But finally… BUZZ!

"Hello?"

"Is this Mrs. Heather Morris?"

"Yes."

"We are unblinding every participant in the Phase 3 trial. According to our records you received…"

With a few words, I was unblinded. And with a few words, I was able to see a future for our world tinged with hope.

Final note: I received two placebo doses in the Phase 3 trial of the Pfizer mRNA vaccine, which commenced in July 2020. As a trial participant, I was subsequently offered two doses of the vaccine, which I hastily accepted. I will continue to be a trial participant, now in the vaccine cohort (almost all participants are now in that group), for the next two years.

Gypsies

Roxanne Lynn Doty
67, Arizona, United States

A green and white trailer sits on Dorsey Street adjacent to Meyer Park, a vintage pull-behind, not longer than twelve feet, no wider than seven, a small dent at the back-right corner. A winter chill has moved into the desert and I briefly forget the long months of traumatic heat, the parched smell of summer, the sun's blinding glare, day after day of suffocating enclosure inside air-conditioned walls. No vehicle is hitched to the trailer. It looks both out of place and parked exactly where it belongs. Tall palm trees shoot into the suburban night sky, streetlights create silhouettes, softly illuminating the neighborhood. The shadow of an olive tree crawls across the sidewalk and up the side of the trailer. An image of the trunk covers the door, branches fan up and outward toward two small windows on either side. Blue curtains hang over one of the windows, a light glows inside.

I walk the perimeter of the park for exercise. Each time I pass the trailer, I try to imagine its story. Why is it here? Who is inside? The light behind the blue curtains makes me think of a mom or dad reading to a child. Maybe this parent lost his or her job, couldn't pay the rent or mortgage, found this quiet neighborhood that seems to offer a safe place to be – for the moment. Maybe the person inside said I quit, just walked away and released themselves from what no longer worked, decided to live differently.

I imagine the owner of the trailer roaming the country, stopping here and there, never settling down, perhaps understanding home differently from those in this quiet, middle-class neighborhood of non-descript ranch-style houses with well-kept lawns and desert-landscapes. Maybe home is a feeling that travels with this person wherever he or she parks the little trailer. A way of being in the world.

When I was a kid we moved around a lot. My brother used to say home was wherever our dad decided to stop the car. My dad would get tired of the place we lived, pack everything we owned in the car and off we'd go. Mostly we wandered between Tennessee and Missouri and New York. Mom called us gypsies. Sometimes she said it with a sigh of resignation, sometimes with a smile. I liked the sound of the word and the idea that there were other people who traveled even more than we did, just took off for dreams of better places. It gave us a place to fit in.

When I was five, my family stayed in a motel in St. Louis for a couple of weeks, one of those single-story motor lodges where you park your car right outside the room's door. My dad couldn't decide where to go next. Luigi's Pizza was just down the street. He said it was the best pizza in the world, even better than New York pizza. He'd drive to Luigi's and come back with dinner. After we ate, he'd go out to the car, sit sideways in the front seat, door open, feet on the parking lot pavement and smoke a cigarette while he poured over the map spread on his lap. He'd study it, as if an answer would come if he looked at it long enough.

On the highways, I thought about people in the other cars and trucks, wondered if they were gypsies, too. The thing I loved most about being a gypsy was the way the road made my dad smile, made him happy which made us all happy as we sailed down the highway, past rest stops and billboards and semi-trucks and exits to new towns and a new life.

The green and white trailer reminds me of the perpetual movement afforded by the road, the impermanence of wherever you are, the comfort of transience. Past and future coalesce into an eternal now as wheels turn on asphalt and the highway's white line races alongside you. Destination is a distant dream, its details can be put off for the moment, arrival a future infinitely deferred, always more perfect than it will turn out to be.

I got the news that my brother was in ICU a few days before Thanksgiving. He had pneumonia. A COVID test was negative, but he required oxygen. My mind went immediately to all the highways that separated us, the long miles between Phoenix, Arizona and Clinton, Missouri where the hospital was located and nearby Warsaw where he and my sister-in-law lived. I thought I should go. Flying was out of the question. I got out my old Rand McNally Travel Atlas and mapped the journey. Four hundred miles from Phoenix to Albuquerque, over 500 from Albuquerque to Oklahoma City, another 400 to Clinton. I thought of pee stops, stops for gas, for food, at least two nights in a motel, maybe three. I thought of Midwestern snowstorms and white outs and COVID-infested air. Mostly, I thought of my brother and how much I loved him.

When we were kids, the world was right if he was around. My brother was seven years older than me. He was right next to me when I got my first kitten, my first day at school. On Halloweens, he took me and my sister trick or treating before he went with his friends, made sure the brown grocery bags we carried were full of treats before he brought us back home. He walked with me to school when I was in first grade and he was in eighth. Our first Christmas on Long Island when our parents had very little money, he was seventeen and worked at Korvettes, a precursor to stores like Target. He bought most of the gifts that year, bought the tree, made sure we had a nice holiday. I was ten when he left Long Island. Our family was fragile, broken in ways I was too young to understand. I remember how sad I was, the gaping hole in our shattered family. Many years passed before I saw him again.

My brother lay in the small rural hospital in Clinton, Missouri for a week. Antibiotics were not working. A doctor came down from Kansas City, said he needed to be moved to a better hospital there. But no ICU beds were available. Rural hospitals throughout the state were sending their COVID patients into Kansas City. Hospitals were overflowing. A day passed and miraculously a bed became available at Research Medical Center. They took him by ambulance, a two-hour drive. My sister-in-law couldn't go. She hadn't been allowed to see him since he was admitted to the hospital in Clinton. I was still in Phoenix, my sister in the Twin Cities. We talked about trying to get to Missouri, the risks of traveling during the pandemic, what we could possibly do when we got there. The doctor who got my brother into Research Medical Center had the exact same name as my deceased father. I took that as a sign, as if my dad was a force in the afterlife come back to save his son. Of course, it made no sense, a ridiculous thought.

I imagined a miracle drug racing through my brother's veins, a stream of pure healing. I thought of victims of COVID and their families, how loved ones could not be near one another, the massive tragedy thrust upon so many. I thought of the long, curving driveway to my brother's place in Warsaw. All through the hellish summer I'd thought of when it was safe, I'd drive to the Twin Cities to visit my sister, stop in Warsaw on the way and visit my brother. I saw the sign at the end of the winding drive approaching his house that read: *Mike's Place*.

I could not fathom a world without him.

By the time I've walked the perimeter of Meyer Park for the sixth time, the light behind the blue curtain is out, the trailer dark. The park is quiet, the kiddy playground empty, basketball players gone. I picture someone sleeping peacefully inside the trailer.

Our family spread out across the country. Sometimes the miles separating us seemed impossible. But we became strong, our core thick. After my dad died, we had a reunion every year. Those days together were enormous. After my mom died, we carried on the reunion, sometimes with our grown kids, sometimes just us. The green and white trailer makes me think it might have been nice if we had one to pull behind our car on all those highways so long ago. We could have slept in it instead of the motels. It would have been crowded, but the motel rooms were pretty crammed, too. I never minded. It felt cozy. I long for that feeling again.

The next night, the trailer is gone. I was hoping it would stay longer. It opened to a world far from the suburban neighborhood, beyond this long-lasting moment that has thrust me into the dark, like those amusement park rides where you sit in a capsule-shaped enclosure speeding through blackness on tracks that seem to hover in the ether. This ungraspable time has deposited a deep sorrow in my bones. I want desperately to break through time and space, touch the parallel world of yesterdays when death was far away, those I loved firmly anchored next to me, so close, breathing each other's air, taking ourselves and one another for granted, never giving our attachment a second thought. I breathe in loss and mourn those who graced me with their presence for mere seconds like fleeting flashes of lightening.

My brother spent several days in the hospital in Kansas City. A second COVID test was negative, but they still didn't know what was wrong besides pneumonia or why antibiotics were not working. His heart rate was low, then it was high, his brain was not communicating with the rest of his body. They moved him from Emergency ICU to Neural ICU. They did other tests. Results would not come quickly. The doctor said it would be 48-72 hours. My sister-in-law sent an email. She had spoken with him on the phone, told him she loved him. He was able to mutter back that he loved her. I thought this was good news, a sign he might be turning the corner. Still, no test results. An hour after I got her email, she called. The doctor told her to get into the hospital, immediately. My brother wasn't going to make it. He died before she got there.

My brother's test results did not come until several days after his death. Sepsis. His body's response to infection had attacked its own organs and he went into shock. I will forever believe that in the absence of the pandemic and overflowing hospitals and delays in test results, things would have gone differently. He would still be alive.

I have photos of him all over my house. In one, he's holding me up, his arms around my waist. I was a year old. In another, we're standing on a frozen pond in a park in New York. I'm three, he's ten. He's holding my hand, we both look cold. My mind keeps coming back to my plan to drive to Warsaw when COVID is over, down the long driveway to his place. I imagine he'll be there and life will be back to normal.

I received an email from my brother, Labor Day weekend 2020. "I hope you are having a nice holiday," he said. "We're in the hot tub having a couple of beers, listening to Kris Kristofferson, forgetting all the crap of the world." It was still blazing hot in Phoenix. I wanted time to pass quickly so the weather would cool. I longed for fall and winter. But my brother was alive then and I would give anything to stop time back in September 2020, to transport myself to Warsaw, Missouri, have my sister there with us, sit in my brother's hot tub, sip beer and listen to Kristofferson. Reminisce about our crazy, dysfunctional family, how despite everything there had always been love.

Two desert willows about ten feet apart in Meyer Park look like skeletons, their branches scrawny and nearly bare. But, on late afternoons in the fleeting space of time just before dusk, the descending sun dazzles intensely, holding on to itself for as long as it can. Before it dies, the sun hits the willows and sets the few remaining leaves ablaze in amber and gold. They flicker briefly as if on fire.

I Wanted to Listen to His Stomach, Not Miss Him

Kaitlyn Pacheco
25, Ohio, United States

Justin and I spent our last pre-pandemic day together alternating between exploring my new Baltimore neighborhood and curling up in my basement sublet. It was the final day of his weekend trip, which, after nearly three years of long-distance dating, never got any easier.

After days of shared meals and laughs and stories and sleep, we started to detach again during the car ride to the airport. But not before one of us asked the question that punctuated the end of every visit: When would we see each other again?

We'd been having this conversation monthly since we graduated from college in 2017. After four years of sleepovers in twin XL beds and dates in quiet corners of the library, we accepted our diplomas and prepared to start our adult lives apart, but together. I was heading to a magazine fellowship; he was starting a news-broadcasting job three hours away. On the eve of graduation, we slept on the roof of his apartment, letting only the stars witness our goodbyes.

Somewhere along the way, Justin and I had gotten in the habit of "diagnosing" each other's stomachaches by jokingly resting above the person's belly button to investigate the rumbles and gurgles beneath the surface. Sometimes this tradition was a joke – a silly game to determine how many IPAs we drank the night before. Other times it was a serious request.

We never really acknowledged that this habit had become a part of our relationship, but instead let it quietly become as natural of a gesture as a forehead kiss or a shoulder squeeze. During that final weekend together in Baltimore, Justin listened to my stomach after a marathon day of eating at practically every cafe and bar we passed, not knowing that those same places would be shuttered within a few days.

By mid-March, every text and phone call became more panic-stricken than the last. Along with the rest of the world, Justin and I were instructed to work from home while the country folded in on itself. In those initial days when a "quick shutdown" was the party line of the administration, we jumped at the chance to shelter in place together at his one-bedroom apartment in Columbus, Ohio.

The first two weeks felt like a fever dream. We were terrified by the coronavirus and its mounting consequences, but at the same time, we couldn't help but revel in a short staycation inside his 700 square-foot space. We could finally dedicate hours to activities that we had forgone during our quick weekend trips, like experimenting with new recipes and binge watching the same TV show. I usually didn't bother to empty my suitcase during our visits, but now it felt exciting to see our toiletries stacked next to one another on the bathroom shelf. For the first time in three years, we didn't know when our next goodbye would be, and until then, we filled every minute we could.

As the weeks wore on, we started to act out the "couple behaviors" that we'd been missing out on. We couldn't wait to go grocery shopping, taking turns pushing the cart and laughing beneath our masks. On Facetime calls with our families, we joked about making our first cleaning schedule, mostly in an attempt to keep the conversations light.

Meanwhile, I set up a workspace outside his kitchen to continue my assignments as a magazine editor. We settled into a makeshift schedule: I worked for a few hours before he woke up for his afternoon web-producing shift, and then I kept him company as he posted articles to his TV station's website late into the night. But by the fourth week, I started to stress about the money wasted on my vacant basement sublet.

When my editor unexpectedly called one morning in mid-April, I answered the phone with a whisper to avoid waking Justin in the next room. As the voice on the other side of the line explained that I was being furloughed with no return date, my initial thought was, at least I'm not alone for this.

Suddenly our future in the apartment seemed as uncertain as the world outside of it. Without a clear direction, I spent weeks in an endless cycle of applying for jobs, crying on the couch, and doom-scrolling through social media. Some days, Justin pulled me out of an emotional spiral, other times he gave me space to grieve the loss of the first job I ever loved. In years past, we had adjusted to supporting each other through constant texts and calls, but now we fell back into the comfort of each other's arms and presence.

We started and ended the long summer in limbo. We kept circling around the same question: After the pandemic ended, would I return to Baltimore, leave for a job in a new city, or stay in

Columbus? Even though the apartment had slowly become ours, I couldn't risk putting down roots in case I had to leave again. While we waited for the other shoe to drop, the suitcase that I packed in March remained in its original spot on the floor of Justin's room.

Without knowing how much time we had left as roommates, we tried to make the most of every day in quarantine. On Fridays, we made elaborate breakfasts together, piling four plates of food on a two-person table. In between movie marathons and puzzle sessions, we spent hours talking through issues we had avoided confronting during our monthly visits.

Meanwhile, my days revolved around online job postings and the pages-long spreadsheet that tracked the progress of my applications. My anxiety rose and fell based on the status of the red spreadsheet cells that represented everything from rejection emails to the painful "ghosting" experiences.

When the additional federal unemployment funding dried up, I applied to any job that I could find, regardless of whether or not I could picture myself working in that position. Justin and I coped with the constant unknowns by celebrating with takeout food when a job interview went well, and crying together when opportunities passed me by.

When my sublease ended, I drove back to Baltimore to repack the dusty clothes and furniture that hadn't been touched in months. My parents stored my mattress in their basement as we waited to find out which city it would travel to next. By then, the emotional toll of our situation felt too heavy to explain to other people, and I started to leave texts from friends and family unanswered.

As summer turned to fall, Justin's lease renewal deadline loomed over our heads. I spent hours scrolling through Zillow, imagining the places we could live if and when I found a job. But in reality, our future in Columbus hinged upon whether I got one, both, or neither of the offers I was waiting to hear back about. With one position based in New York and the other remote-friendly, we tried to prepare ourselves to revert back to monthly visits and nightly calls.

During the days that we spent waiting for an answer, I felt the same sadness that I always associated with driving Justin to the airport. That constant, dull pain of knowing that our time together was about to end, but wanting to make those last seconds, minutes, and hours count. As many times as we tried to brace one another by repeating the mantras "We've done this before" and "We can make it work again," we knew this time was different. Our quarantine experience had given us a glimpse at what our future could be like, and it hurt even more to know exactly what we'd be walking away from.

And then, on one of the last humid days of the year, I answered another call with a whisper. This time, when I hung up the phone, I ran outside to find Justin in his usual spot on the front porch. We liked to take turns reading in a beat-up rocking chair that sat in a sliver of sunlight, and when he turned toward me and smiled, I knew we would never live apart again.

Later that night, we returned home from celebrating with too much wine and pasta and fell into bed. We smiled at the ceiling, knowing that everything and nothing had changed that day. When my stomach groaned under the weight of our festivities, Justin grinned, lifted the edge of my shirt, and leaned down to rest his ear on my belly button.

Chop Wood, Carry Water

Anne Gudger
61, Oregon, United States

Before enlightenment, chop wood, carry water. After enlightenment, chop wood, carry water.

– Zen proverb

"Are you two okay?" our daughter asked when I answered my cell. Worry inked her voice.

I started to say yes, we're okay, but she interrupted. "Where are you? I-5 North just closed. Eugene through Salem is pure smoke," she said. "Please don't stop for anything."

"We're okay," I said again, searching the still blue sky for any smoky wisps that could turn to walls of gray smoke. The inside of our car smelled like a road trip: empty coffee cups, potato chips, melted Reese's cups – even a cheeseburger from our recent stop in Yreka, California.

"No problem," my husband said. "We can pop off I-5 and take 99 through Ashland."

It was September 8th and wildfires ripped through California and Oregon. We'd managed to avoid the California fires when we visited our son and daughter-in-law in Irvine just a few days ago. We thought we were ahead of the Oregon fires.

As we snaked through Ashland, Oregon, Highway 99 closed. We became part of a car chain, all these metal links slithering left and right. We couldn't go north. We couldn't go south. Our GPS turned us in circles with rerouting, rerouting. When we recognized cars coming toward us (Is that the same red Suburban? Is that the same Amazon Prime truck?) panic bloomed in my chest.

"We can go to the coast," my husband said. My there's-always-another-way husband.

We're heading to the coast, I texted our son in California, and our daughter in Oregon.

The coast is burning too! Our son texted back with a picture of flames from a news feed. *Don't go. Stay where you are.*

I'll book you a room online, our daughter said.

"Let's pull over and check the news," one of us said.

"And find a bathroom." That was me.

We pulled into the parking lot of a small business where a guy in dusty cargo shorts and a navy T-shirt let me use the bathroom. Then we plopped on the bench outside his front door as we scrolled through the news, as we made and remade plans, as we pretended we could go home that night.

"You probably can't get out," an EMT told us.

She was staged with her crew in the parking lot. In the distance, black smoke boiled in the sky from two trailer parks burning north of Ashland.

"Can you tell me anything?" I asked her.

"Talent and Phoenix are evacuating," she said and pointed her chin towards the charcoal sky. "I have family in Talent," she added, a hiccup in her steady voice. "I'm trying to navigate them out." She swallowed hard and listened to her radio as a dispatcher broadcasted an update. "You're not going to get out. Not tonight."

Talent and Phoenix. Just north of Ashland. Even as it burned, I wanted to believe Phoenix would live up to its name and reform, rise from its ashes. I wanted to believe Ashland wouldn't turn into a land of ash.

We were lucky that night. After an hour of being turned away from motels and hotels. After the sleep shelter the Red Cross set up was full. After thinking we were going to sleep near the park where we'd seen people pitching tents, we finally found a room. When we showed up minutes later, the owner said, "Good thing you told me your name. I had three calls right after you." The anxiety that had stitched itself around my chest, squeezing me with sticky tendrils for the past two hours, melted a little. I tightened the blinds and slept in that delicious bed.

Early the next morning, with I-5 open, we downed a quick cup of coffee and headed home to Banks, Oregon, just outside of Portland.

I studied the papaya sky that cradled the sun to remember I'm big and small in the same breath. I named colors like I do. The sun, a red jawbreaker. The sky in shades of gray – dove, concrete, steel. My beautiful green soggy state. Not green. Not soggy. On fire. Cocooned in smoke. Smoke slinked into everything – hair, clothes, pages of books. That familiar smell of summer evenings, campfires, s'mores. And this was not that. It was the feeling of fear. Of numb.

On the road, I cried monsoon tears. My throat shrank, clogged with a peach pit as we steered past the two trailer parks completely burned. Black outlines of trailers. Charred remains. Jagged tree stumps with molten edges glowing. Smoldering earth that had been people's yards. Where is home when the place you lived is ripped from you? Where is home when you raced ahead of blistering flames with no time to pack a go-bag? When you were lucky to get out still breathing. Or maybe you were lucky and you managed to snatch some piece of art, books, grandma's quilt, the file with passports, wills, mortgage papers. A million acres burned in Oregon. More than 2,300 homes were destroyed. Six people died.

My husband and I landed on the lucky side this time. And on the lucky side the need to help consumed me.

What could we do in the heartbreak?

While we were driving through smoke and sending wishes for safety to everyone caught in the fires, our daughter and son-in-law offered shelter on our farm for anyone who needed it. Our first evening home, two pigs arrived, all grunts and snorts. We nicknamed them Oreo One and Oreo Two on account of their marbled skin. Soon they rooted in a horse stall with an outside run. "They don't do steps," their owner said, eyeing the one low-rise step from inside to outside. By the time their drip water system was attached to a hose, they'd mastered the step and the swinging half-door. They wiggled their curly tails and flipped their pig snouts each time I said, "Hi, piggies."

"Anyone else coming tonight?" I asked my daughter as the pigs settled in, fires blazed, and more evacuations were ordered.

"Not yet," she said, squinting at where the sun should be.

We shoveled more stalls clean to be ready.

The next morning horse trainers called. Goat owners called. My daughter and her husband said yes and yes and yes until we were full, until all we could offer were outside horse runs. Even after the barn was full, we took in four more goats that arrived in the back of a new Suburban. They made a temporary home in our oversized, fabric-covered dog kennel where they bleated just outside our bedroom window.

"Who needs sleep?" I said.

I woke the next morning to not day and not night. I woke to the inside of a cloud – or rather, the inside of a chimney. Breathed air that was the worst quality in the world. September 13th, Portland topped out at 516 on the Air Quality Index – a scale that only goes up to 500. Portland rocketed ahead of Delhi, India (157), Karachi, Pakistan (142) and Kuwait City, Kuwait (117). I wanted to hold my breath as if holding could rescue my lung sacs, my bronchi that stretch and reach and quiver like the branches of naked trees.

Chop wood, carry water. My mantra in a loop since the fires struck. A shortened version of the Zen quote: "Before enlightenment, chop wood, carry water. After enlightenment, chop wood, carry water."

I want to ink it on my skin. This reminder. Small steps. Keep moving. Rest when rest is needed. Be kind. Love your beloveds. Cook good food. Shovel poop. Boil herbs to improve the air. Breathe deep in between.

Our quiet farm now bustled with trailers in our parking lot where people slept to be close to their horses, to stay safe from their homes. Trucks and trailers pulling up, pulling through. The one driver swearing because she couldn't make the turn and had to back up; because sometimes you have to go backwards to go forward. The scuff of extra muck boots on gravel. Strangers hauling feed and blankets. Strangers pushing wheelbarrows topped with hay, piled with manure. That one wheelbarrow with its squeaky wheel. My family and I took comfort in the sounds in the chaos. In the voices of humans saying, "Hi" and "We're okay" and "Thank you."

Doing something still felt galaxies better than sinking into the numb. All of those visitors were a heart balm. Our daughter opened our barn doors to strangers and sheltered seventeen horses, nine goats, and two pigs. Twenty-eight extra hearts thrummed on our farm. One hundred and twelve extra legs. One hundred and twelve extra hooves. Stomping, resting, standing, sleeping, digging. Hearts pumping. Breathing here while they waited to breathe back home.

Guess Who?

Ashlee Petrucci
39, Alberta, Canada

I squint my eyes at the photos and cock my head, as though altering my sightline will make it easier to identify the students with their royal blue gowns, lipstick, and fresh smiles; their carefully combed and styled hair. Our high school Graduation Committee had sent a PowerPoint to staff in an effort to properly identify and label photos of this year's graduating class. I flip through the slides several times. First, as a personal test to see how many student names I can guess correctly, then a few more to torture myself with the fact that I fail to recognize grade twelves who sit a mere ten feet away within my own classroom.

Perplexed, I sit back and stare at the screen. Why can't I recognize these kids? The answer comes immediately: after several months of teaching these students in masks, their faces without them have become unrecognizable.

As a child, my favorite game was Guess Who?, a character guessing game consisting of two boards, each the size of a laptop, that contain a series of flip-up frames with pictures of people. Each player (there are only two) picks a character then asks a series of yes or no questions to determine their opponent's identity, all of which are based on physical appearance. As you proceed through the questions, you eliminate the wrong characters by flipping down their frames, leaving at the end, one correct answer, hopefully.

This school year has been the ultra-marathon of Guess Who? and these graduation photos merely solidify my feelings. I hate masks and the board game I loved as a child was much easier than the reality-show version. I've become reliant on seating charts and mastered the art of reading eyes because I've had very few other indicators to gauge student well-being. In fact, when the eyes fail, I've resorted to "thumbs up or thumbs down?" in order to assess general class feeling.

Nevertheless "thumbs up or thumbs down" won't help me identify students, so I accept the fact I only recognize two (with a couple more hypotheses) and move on with my day.

As my next class filters into the room, the routine is all too familiar: the first student kindly splatters sanitizer on all the desks, while the others sanitize their hands, grab paper towels, then clean their workspace. Their dedication to cleanliness has been remarkable and largely unwavering, even after months of similar routines in all their classes.

I remove my mask, thankful for the freedom to do-so when instructing from the front of the room. This has saved the students from hours of Charlie Brown teacher noises when reading *Hamlet*, which needs no further complication beyond its already-challenging Elizabethan English.

"Good afternoon everyone! How are we doing today?" I survey the class. Many students nod and offer a thumbs-up, while others respond in muffled facemask tones, "Good, Ms. P. You?"

"I'm doing pretty well today. Absolutely thrilled of course to keep reading *Hamlet*…" I pause for effect, giving the class an opportunity to roll their eyes, although to be honest, this group is scarily academic.

"Alright then, let's decide on readers. We're tackling Act II, Scene ii so I need Polonius, Reynaldo, and Ophelia. Any volunteers?" The hands pop-up quickly, as do voices not connected to hands.

"I'll be Polonius!"

I glance around the room in search of the voice's owner, "Was that you Cameron?"

"Nope. Think it was Aarish."

I raise my eyes to Aarish near the back, who raises his hands in confusion, "Sorry Ms. P, not me, but I'll be Reynaldo."

"Sure, that's fine." I write Aarish's name on the board beside Reynaldo and in the back of my mind, curse the fact that with these masks, I struggle to associate voices with bodies because I can't see mouths move.

"So, who was it that wanted to read Polonius? Please raise your hand; you know how difficult it is to hear with these masks." No one moves. Apparently my round of Guess Who?, the voice recognition version, has terrified the brave volunteer so I select Jay to read Polonius, then Eve to read Ophelia.

"Okay, before we begin, take a few minutes to review the study guide questions while I take attendance."

The students quickly access the document online as I survey the class. There are a few empty seats today and I input the absent names into the school system. I barely glance at my seating chart, feeling confident in my ability to identify the students with factors beyond facial recognition, using clues such as hairstyle, clothing, and height. Students that frequently participate in class are easy to remember; those that enter quietly and leave even more silently, are difficult. I press "submit" then pick up my copy of *Hamlet* so we can begin.

It's clear that I'm playing a losing game because within seconds of uploading the attendance into our school server, a hand shoots up.

"Ms. P, I'm here, but you've marked me as absent."

I follow the hand and voice to a male student in the second-last row.

"Oh, sorry. I'll fix that." The student lowers his head so that only straight black hair is visible.

I mumble under my breath, thinking to myself – damn it, who is this? There are six boys who sit together, all of whom are of Asian descent. Having taught two of them before, I've had no trouble identifying either of them in masks, but the four new students have caused challenges. Unfortunately, they all have short dark hair, dress similarly, and speak very little. Two of the six are absent and while I know neither is a former student, I'm not sure which of the new students I've misidentified. Not everyone is so diligent with their attendance being marked correctly, so I can't assume entries from earlier classes are correct.

I open the computer to their class photos. The students have a tendency to switch spots so I can't rely on my seating chart. I can narrow it down to either Keith or Tim because neither wears glasses, but I need something else to go on. I regard each photo carefully and then study the student in question. Hair color and hairstyle are already out. Eyes are tricky, especially at the moment with the student staring at their phone.

My stomach lurches and my face feels hot. What am I going to do? How do I fix this? At this point in the semester, I can't ask for the student's name. While the circumstances are unusual with masks covering significant identifiers, to ask for a student's name halfway through the semester is like breaking a cardinal rule – you simply don't. A teacher should know. A teacher must know.

I decide to wander through the class, to fake "checking-up" on the students and whether they are indeed reviewing the study guide. (Although, with attendance taking this long, my ruse will only result in uncovering various games, texts, and Instagram perusals.) I hope that I might catch the student's name on a handout or…okay, I haven't a clue, but it's my first option.

I wander slowly up-and-down the rows, nodding at students, ignoring their quick screen switches between texts to schoolwork. I arrive at the student-in-question to discover nothing on his desk besides his copy of *Hamlet* and a pencil.

Defeated, I return to my desk and stare once more at the class list. I know there has to be another way, a more effective way to correct my error and just when I'm ready to abandon attendance, to move-on with this very tardy lesson, I spot a pile of completed marking that I haven't returned.

It's brilliant. Rather than hand out the work, I'll call the students' names and have them pick-up their assignments from my desk.

"Sorry to interrupt everyone, but before we begin reading, I'd like to return your advice columns. When I call your name, please come pick-up your work."

I move quickly through the names then arrive at name one of two, "Tim?" The student-in-question doesn't budge. "Keith?" For a moment no movement, and my panic returns until his friend elbows him, "Dude – Ms. P just called your name." I smile widely and hand Keith his work as he approaches my desk.

"You're going to fix my attendance, right?"

"Yes, Keith, right now."

With relief, I update the attendance and pick-up my copy of *Hamlet*, finally ready to begin class. While I know that an attendance error isn't the end of the world, I hate the fact that a mask made it impossible for me to identify a student. Not just any student, but one of *my* students. I take great pride in knowing each of them not just by name, but also, by their smiles and facial expressions. This is one game of Guess Who? that I could easily do without.

Aftershocks

Duygu Eyrenci
29, Izmir, Turkey

When the rumors about a deadly virus in Wuhan, China started circulating on the internet, I was celebrating my admittance into a graduate program in the United States. I had earned my bachelor's degree in American Studies in 2013, and it had taken me six years to muster up the courage to study abroad. A college experience ruined by bullies had left me with a deep mistrust for society in general. Among those bullies, perhaps the one I shared a dorm room with for only two months had the most scathing and permanent effect on my life. Sharing a tiny room with a person who I knew hated me, having no space of my own to hide from her ever-judging gaze and just to be myself in peace, worrying about every small mistake I might make, and walking on eggshells all the time... such a cruel living arrangement takes a toll on you. The feeling didn't go away, even after I switched roommates.

By the time I graduated, I was mentally drained. I returned to my hometown, Izmir, where I had the chance to live alone. I found a job as a freelance copywriter because I was too scared to have co-workers and navigate the notorious office politics. I learned to cut my own hair so that I wouldn't have to worry about the small talk with the hairdresser. I learned to cook so that I wouldn't have to interact with the delivery person. Gyms were scary places that put me in a self-conscious mood, so I built a decent home workout routine. I didn't travel because unfamiliar places were too overwhelming. I rarely went out to see friends. The power of holding the keys to my apartment and knowing I could shut the world out whenever I wanted, as long as I wanted, was almost intoxicating. And once I was ready to break my addiction to that power, 2020 happened.

At first, I was optimistic. I thought COVID-19 would be another outbreak that would die down on its own before it could hinder my plans in any way. Even when it became obvious that this disease was different, it didn't faze me much. I felt mentally ready to become an international student, but an extra year to build up even more confidence didn't seem too bad either. I already worked from home, knew how to cook my own food, bake my own bread, and cut my own hair. I had acquired several hobbies I could do alone at home over the past six years. I had a long list of books to read and movies to watch. I had a support network of online friends from all over the world, so I didn't feel socially isolated either. Staying at home wasn't a challenge – it was my area of expertise. I had been preparing for a pandemic without knowing it. I was happy and comfortable, and I knew how lucky I was to be able to say that.

That was, until October 30, 2020.

I was sitting at my desk, chatting with a friend from the UK when the earthquake started.

At first, I wasn't too worried. There hadn't been any of them recently, but I was used to earthquakes. We experienced several almost every year. They were a part of our day-to-day life. I knew quite a number of destructive earthquakes had been recorded in the history of Izmir. As the tremors grew more violent instead of abating, I realized this earthquake was different. This was going to be a catastrophe. As I squatted next to my bed and waited helplessly, I thought I might have finally run out of luck.

I am not sure when exactly it stopped because earthquakes leave people with shaky legs and dizziness for some time, but there came a hopeful moment when the tremors ceased to seem never-ending. As the tremors subsided, I grabbed my phone and called my family to set up a meeting location. Not long after that the phone lines went down. I packed up several essential items, including face masks and hand sanitizer, and left the apartment. For as long as I could remember, we had been advised to keep an "earthquake bag" at the ready and determine a rendezvous point with our loved ones. Like most people, we never had, foolishly and arrogantly thinking we would never need them. We thought we were immune to tragedies, that they were for other people, nameless people we would never know in person, even when literally the whole world was being threatened by a deadly virus.

The neighbors were hurrying past me down the stairs as I locked the door. Oddly enough, I was shutting my apartment out for a change, already dreading the inevitable moment I would have to go back in there. The world outside felt much safer than home now. On my way to the rendezvous point, I saw people gathered on the streets, in the parks. No one cared about social distancing anymore. I didn't blame them. I wasn't big on physical contact myself, but I knew they needed some form of comfort. We were a people who lived in a country prone to seismic activities and had witnessed many earthquakes. We had seen streets turned into mass graveyards on the news. It was quite possible some of those people had seen such sights in person – a possibility that hadn't occurred to me up until that day. I didn't spot any damaged buildings myself, but soon, sirens and helicopters could be heard in the distance.

Indeed, we were right to fear. It was an earthquake with a magnitude of 6.9-7.0 that had struck under the Aegean Sea. A tsunami had also hit some of the coastal towns. One hundred and seventeen people had died and more than 1,000 people had been injured in Turkey. In Greece, two people had died and 19 had been injured. As it happens. It was the deadliest earthquake of 2020. In the following weeks, there was also a significant increase in the COVID-19 cases in Izmir. Again, my family and I were lucky. Our homes weren't damaged and we owned a vacation house we could stay in while waiting out the most intense of the aftershocks for the following two weeks. We had to take public transport to get there since we didn't have a car, but none of us showed any COVID-19 symptoms later.

After two weeks, I was ready to go back to my normal life, or rather, "the new normal." The aftershocks had been predicted to be the strongest and most frequent during the first ten days following the earthquake, but they didn't completely stop even after that. I was back to feeling on edge all the time, for an entirely different reason. Home should be the place where everyone feels safe, where nothing can harm us; but even this is not always true. What can we do, if our homes fail us during a time when we need them the most? Be it a devastating earthquake, a lethal virus, or a toxic roommate? Where else can we hide safely other than a place that we can confidently call our own? That is a privilege we often take for granted.

I hope 2020 has made people rethink the concept of "home" and what it truly stands for. It has made me realize how easily home can be taken for granted, even when we appreciate its protection a bit too much sometimes.

Thanksgiving 2020

Christine DiNovis Leonard
43, Pennsylvania, United States

It was Friday, November 20, 2020, and I was on the floor of our hallway, gasping for air. I was nauseous, too, and the room was starting to spin. My son, Danny, ran over.

"Get my inhaler," I croaked. He grabbed it out of my purse at the bottom of the steps. I pulled myself up and huffed it, the albuterol tingled on my tongue. I could breathe again, but the nausea was getting worse.

"Danny, you're going to have to drive me to the Urgent Care," I told him. He looked at me, startled. He'd only gotten his permit a few months ago. "Your dad's out with your sisters and I'm too sick to drive myself."

"Okay." I held onto him as I stumbled to the car. When we got to the Urgent Care, Danny had to park on the side of the building. A nurse came out from a side door and I left my son in the car as I staggered toward the bright lights. After the nurse took my vitals I sat in an orange chair in the tiny room, a sliding door barricading me from the hallway. Nausea rolled over me again, and I began to shake and sweat. I couldn't stay upright in the

163

orange chair and crawled onto the examining table instead. When the doctor came in, I was in a fetal position.

"I'm so sorry you're not feeling well," she said. "Do you know if you've been exposed to anyone with COVID?"

"I don't know for sure, but I teach in a high school, so it's very possible," I said.

"Got it. We're going to do a test for COVID, but unfortunately, given your symptoms, I would guess that you will be positive," she said, preparing the swab.

The worst-case scenario. I was an overweight woman in my forties with an autoimmune disorder and asthma to boot. COVID could kill me.

"Are you able to sit up?" the doctor asked. I pushed myself up. "Try to tip your head back, please." I winced as she pushed a long swab into my nose. I'd been tested for COVID a month earlier (negative), but that swab had felt like it was piercing my brain. This one, thankfully, was not as invasive.

"All done. You should have your results within 3-5 days. You can take ibuprofen for pain. Make sure to stay hydrated and to rest as much as possible. I will give you a paper that will let your school know that you can't return to work until your test results come back."

I took the paperwork and walked slowly back to the car. I put my head on the cool window and closed my eyes as Danny drove me home.

Two days later. No results yet. I'd moved to our downstairs guest room to quarantine from my husband and four children. Life was a blur of coughing, sleeping, looking for "air pockets" as I called them in my haze. If I stayed very still on my side, I could breathe better. My friend had sent me a pulse oximeter, which stayed on my finger like a bizarre ring. It was usually within the normal range. That evening I dragged myself to the shower, hoping that the steam might open my airways. When I got out, I realized that I smelled nothing. I pumped soap onto my hand and put it to my nose. Nothing. I opened a small bottle of bleach sitting next to the washing machine. Nothing. I couldn't smell my fear, either, but it permeated the room.

The next day I received the message:

SARS CoV-2 PCR	Detected	A
A Detected result is considered a positive test result for COVID-19. This indicates that RNA from SARS-CoV-2 [formerly 2019-nCoV] was detected, and the patient is infected with the virus and presumed to be contagious.		

Almost a week had passed since my doctor's visit. It was my twelfth trip back from the bathroom that night. I'd been having unrelenting, bloody, diarrhea for hours. I was shaking, and terrified. My husband, who had also been diagnosed with COVID, had been checking on me, but had fallen asleep upstairs. I was going to die, and I didn't know what to do. At 2 a.m. I called my family practice's answering service. I was told that I would receive a call back from a doctor within a half an hour. I sat in the living room, huddled under blankets in the "comfy chair" as my girls had dubbed it, crying softly. I pinned my hopes on what the doctor would tell me. Surely there was a medication I could take that would fix these symptoms. I'd been on a diet of ibuprofen, zinc, and hot tea. The ibuprofen seemed to help the most. Minutes clicked by. I prayed. I contemplated. I cried some more.

When I spoke to the doctor on call, she sounded young. I explained my symptoms and her response was, "That's not normal." No kidding. "You should go to the ER right away." I agreed and hung up, then called my husband.

"Do you want to go now?" This question reminded me of the trips to the hospital we'd made together when our babies were going to be born. This time, however, there was no baby, and no excitement.

"Not yet," I said. He snuggled up next to me and held me. We lay like that for a bit, and then I struggled into new clothes and put on my sneakers. It was time to go.

In the car I'd started to feel a little better. I walked into the ER, supported by my husband. They placed a hospital bracelet on my wrist.

"I'm okay," I said. "Just head home to the kids."

"No, I'll stay."

"You're sick, too. I'll be okay. Seriously," I gave him a wan smile.

"Alright, but keep me posted. Is your phone charged?" I assured him that it was. As I waited to be called back to triage, I began to feel worse. The dizziness was upon me again, and staying upright became harder. By the time I was called in, I was zigzagging down the hallway, following the nurse. She grabbed my arm and helped me onto the bed. A shuddering darkness came over me and I moaned in pain. I couldn't breathe, couldn't speak – I was going to throw up, or pass out, or both.

Suddenly there were multiple people in the room, but my vision was blurry and I closed my eyes.

"Stay with me!" someone yelled while someone else pulled off my shirt and began to stick circles onto my skin.

"Come on, stick with us!" This from another voice. I couldn't talk; all I could do was groan. Usually I'd be embarrassed to be so exposed, but I couldn't care. Nothing mattered. I wasn't even scared. I just wanted the pain to stop.

"Get her an IV!" Someone stuck my limp hand and attached the IV drip. Minutes or hours passed. I fell asleep.

When I awoke, the room was dark.

"Wow, I can't believe you slept this long without having to get up to use the restroom," a nurse said. "We filled you with two bags of fluids."

"I feel a lot better," I told her.

"That's so good to hear. I'll let the doctor know you're awake."

Several minutes later the doctor came in. I sat up a bit to talk to him.

"Well, it's great to see you doing better."

"Yeah. I'm alright now."

"You had hypertension due to hypovolemia," he said. I rolled the terms around in my brain, trying to make sure to remember them. "I'll tell you the truth: you had me scared. I'm so glad that you're doing well now."

His statement shocked me. I knew how horrible I'd felt a few hours before, but the realization that I had worried a doctor was terrifying. It meant I'd been close to death. For real. This wasn't even ODS (Overly-Dramatic-Syndrome), a phrase coined by my kids for their dramatic mom.

"You'll be discharged soon. Just keep hydrating and call your family doctor to follow up."

Wait a minute. He's sending me home?

"The ER has been really crazy today. You're my fifth COVID patient of the day. And it's just me and two other doctors."

My husband came to pick me up. He looked ill, too, although his symptoms had not been as severe as mine. I told him what had happened.

"I'm so glad that you're okay."

"Yeah, me too." There weren't many words for all of the emotions I was feeling. Mostly, though, I was just tired. When we got home, I remembered that it was Thanksgiving Day. My children had cooked a feast: a perfectly browned turkey, stuffing, mashed potatoes, gravy, green bean casserole, sweet potatoes with mini marshmallows resting on the top, and biscuits. I couldn't smell a thing, but it didn't matter. I was home, alive, with my family, and my thankfulness was abundant.

Hope is the Special Tonight

Michael Cannistraci
63, New York, United States

We huddled inside the plywood shelter, bundled in our gloves and winter coats. Rain glistened on the street and the wind blasted arctic air. We were celebrating my wife's birthday in New York City COVID-19 style, cramped under a space heater, surrounded by wilted majesty palms and dried out mums. The couple next to us, martinis in hand, looked at us warily. I imagined they were estimating the distance between our tables, which was definitely not six feet. The red wine in our glasses became chilled after a few seconds, and the potato leek soup threatened to develop a thin layer of ice.

Our French waiter cracked jokes about the circumstances. Despite the chilly conditions, walk-in customers were turned away. The pandemic had made any dining, including freezing outside, a valued commodity. My wife and I toasted each other and the fact that we were alive.

Just then a woman with a black Labradoodle walked by. Her black cocktail dress was covered front and back with Christmas bows, the kind you tape on the top of presents, and her hem was trimmed in tinsel. She was wearing a Santa hat and the labradoodle had a red electric bow tie that flashed on and off. My wife laughed and I called out to the woman and she stopped and turned around.

I told her how great she looked and we both laughed. The other customers stopped to take her in and laughed as well. She told us she and her friend were out of work as Broadway show people, so they made little boxes of homemade ravioli as gifts to friends and she was going from apartment to apartment, dropping them off. "We have to keep finding some joy in the little things," she said. My wife asked if she could take her picture, she agreed and picked up the dog and struck a pose. We all laughed and the customers outside applauded her as she walked away.

We walked up Amsterdam Ave after dinner, passed people dining and drinking on sidewalk tables, bundled for the cold. I glanced at rows of windows, some lit with Christmas lights. The apartments were filled with people cloistered on an island of eight million people. I reflected on the gift of chance encounters and the comfort of strangers, locked down in isolation. I wondered when those strangers would walk and eat and laugh freely again. The gift of chance encounters and the comfort of strangers was never one I had appreciated.

I do now.

Taco Tuesdays

Terri Elders
84, California, United States

I ignited New Year's Day in 2020 by dropping a match while lighting a pine-scented candle on the bookcase next to my old glider rocker. I scooped up the match and blew out the flicker. But when my ceiling alarm shrieked, I noticed that a spark had landed on my chair's foam cushion. I quickly dragged the smoldering seat onto my balcony and smothered the flames eating the fabric.

I hoped it wasn't an omen. I'd looked forward to a shiny new year.

An hour later, my new friend, Rob, phoned. I'd met him a few months earlier when we were each fresh from breakups of similarly toxic three-year relationships. Saying goodbye to romantic attachments is not an easy transition for two people in their early eighties.

Rob and I shared a mutual love of theater, jazz concerts, museums, art galleries, and movies, so at the onset of our friendship, we'd visited these and began to commemorate Taco Tuesdays.

"Are you up to happy hour next Taco Tuesday?" He asked me. "It's my turn to treat."

Rob labeled himself a "half-assed pescatarian vegan," who shunned meat and dairy, but favored fish or seafood. Lucky for him, fish tacos in this century have become increasingly popular in Southern California.

I agreed to the upcoming Tuesday. We went and had a marvelous time.

By late February, we'd heard rumbles about a new novel coronavirus that had started ravaging certain communities in Northern California, as well as Washington State.

On March 13 we sat squeezed together, a little uneasily, in a tiny local theater, watching a staging of Fitzgerald's "The Great Gatsby." We'd heard earlier that day about a death in California, related to this new disease. We'd made plans to attend an annual St. Patrick's Day singalong that a music teacher I knew had long hosted, but now wondered if it would be safe.

Then, everything changed. The hostess canceled her party, at the urging of her family, so we celebrated the holiday quietly together at Rob's house. He donned his Scots Irish tartan shirt and provided snacks. I fastened my Irish scarf with a lucky leprechaun clip and brought Jameson Irish Whiskey.

Within days, the governor of California declared a state of emergency and issued a series of stay-at-home orders that closed restaurants, except for curbside pickups. Nowhere to go for happy hour anymore.

At this point, I turned once again to literature for comfort and re-read sections of Samuel Pepys's, "Journal of a Plague Year." Pepys's 17th century diary paralleled what we were going through now, I concluded. And just as he had turned to tobacco rolls to stave off melancholy, I realized that those happy hour Taco Tuesdays had helped me keep my spirits up. But what were we to do without restaurants?

Throughout the spring, we met in a public park, not far from his condo, close to the beach. Since everybody huddled inside these days, it felt good to enjoy the early evening breeze, inhale the salty tang of the air, and watch children ride their bikes and skateboards through the park. Strollers passed us, all masked and socially distant.

I contributed a thermos of margaritas and dark chocolate for dessert, and Rob brought fish tacos, chips, and salsa from a cantina he favored. We perched at opposite ends of a park bench, on nippy late-April afternoons, gripping our plastic cups with gloved hands, and grinning between sips and nibbles.

By June, we began to favor the gardens of my senior living complex, splitting a bottle of cabernet sauvignon or a thermos of margaritas, accompanied by take-out fish tacos. By now, I began each morning by checking the previous day's tally of hospital admissions, ICU patients, and newly identified cases in Orange County.

Rob's granddaughter, who worked at a beachside bar, was the first person he knew to come down with COVID. As the weeks rolled by, more and more people we knew reported friends or family sickened. Many survived but developed long-lasting symptoms. My best friend's aunt in Connecticut died of the disease in a nursing home where she'd recently moved. By August the governor eased statewide regulations, and once again Orange County restaurants began offering outside dining. I brightened. I felt as if a ray of long-awaited sunshine had broken through the gloom of despair. Rob and I ventured to new venues to observe our happy hours.

Then one afternoon, I dropped a packet of taco spice mix at the supermarket. When I tried to catch it, I felt a searing pain in my arm.

"Good catch," a customer down the aisle cried out. My arm hurt so much I could scarcely keep from screaming as I loaded my groceries onto the counter so the checker could ring them up. I messaged my primary care physician. She replied that it sounded like a rupture of my right distal biceps at the elbow and told me to go to Urgent Care.

The next day I parked in a handicapped space not far from the entrance and picked my way toward the building. My glasses tend to fog when I wear a mask, so I stopped several times to clear them. I passed by a leafy tree as I approached and then fell, tripping over a raised gap in the pavement caused by growing tree roots. I hurtled to the ground, hit my head in the crosswalk, shattered my glasses, knotted my left eyebrow, bruised my knees – and my spirits. I hadn't seen the crack. The shady branches had obscured it.

I phoned Rob when I got home. "Isn't this enough misfortune?"

"Don't worry," he reassured me. "You can lift your margarita with your left hand until your right arm heals." I managed to giggle.

At our next Taco Tuesday, we toasted to better days.

We'd located a couple of restaurants offering outside tents or makeshift patios. As autumn approached, some owners installed heat lamps so customers could enjoy happy hour specials until

7 p.m. One favorite, a sports bar and pub, hung TVs along the exterior walls, so we watched back-to-back games of the World Series and the NBA championships as we savored our taco treats.

In the chillier air of winter, COVID stuttered and resurged. Rob and I resorted to Skype, meeting online as we hoisted our 5 o'clock happy hour wine or margaritas.

In December Rob decided to sell his condo near me and begin the process of finding and relocating to a new one 25 miles south, in an upscale luxurious senior living complex. Two days before New Year's Eve, we Skyped to toast the incoming year.

Recently I received this email from Rob:

I am sorry that I have not been in contact lately. I have met a woman with whom I am developing a relationship. Consequently, I will not be seeing you any longer. I wish you the very best. Thank you for being a great friend and all of your support and help through these trying times!

When I opened this missive, three weeks had passed since our last shared Taco Tuesday encounter. We'd returned to that old sports bar where we'd watched the Dodgers and Lakers in those playoffs in autumn.

But what an understatement. Trying times, indeed! I'd gained a new habit, so there's some consolation. And at 84, I'd survived my Plague Year, even though it appears I've lost a companion.

Looking ahead, I begin to salivate at the thought of oh, say, a carnitas taco. Why not? As Samuel Pepys observed, "The truth is, I do indulge myself a little more in pleasure, knowing that this is the proper age of my life to do it."

Twice Daily

Angelica Whitehorne
25, New York, United States

That year, that double dooms year, that better-in-hindsight year, I walked the dog from the four different places we lived. The first was our home for over a decade, a squat brick complex with its own secrets. I walked out its front door, leading the dog away from the busy road twice daily; and when the contagion yanked the girl next door from preschool like a tadpole from the bank of a pond, I let her walk the dog with me. A pink mask or a blue mask or a mask with the logo of my workplace or a floral mask that someone else's grandmother sewed for me, adorned on my sweaty face to protect myself from the girl's spit particles, which had always been gross, but could now also be deadly.

We walked down the block, and always stopped at the elderly couple's house, who sat on their porch and gave us perfectly suburban greetings, and smiled at the girl whenever I brought her with me; probably thinking she was adorable, but altogether too much to handle in their old age as she squealed, and asked for a beverage, and told them once again she was four-years-old, but smarter than the other four-years-olds by a whole lot, a whoooole lot!

And once, while the three of us were making front lawn pleasantries, and I was wondering what they'd say if I asked them to be my full-time grandparents, the girl had screamed out in fury, and all of us looked over to her in terror, even the dog, and with her pinhole eyes poking into each one of us, she screamed out, "I AM TOO HOT!" and so we returned home early.

But most days we made light conversation with the couple and moved on, my dog sticking a leg up on their tree, and me apologizing for it – until one day it was just the man shaking his head grimly, his wife's patio chair missing from their front porch – and then I was apologizing for bigger things, the things we try to ward off with a long walk, a steady walk, a responsibility to the dog, and the dog's bladder, and now the tadpole girl; who took to sitting by the window to listen to the outside and make sure she hadn't missed our walk. When you do many things daily and get into a real routine, it starts to seem like life is forever and nothing will change; but then, it changes.

My favorite part of those walks, besides the girl, and the old couple, who eventually was just the old man, was our stops at the Italian shop on the corner, where the owner would give us rainbow and snowball cookies, and thick cheese samples, and olives that made the girl scrunch up her face and spit down at my shoes while the owner just laughed and laughed, saying, "Don't worry, she will grow into it." I couldn't help but wonder whether he meant the taste of olives, or the taste of all the bitter things she would learn to swallow.

But a month after that hard-to-swallow, sweltering day, we had to pack and relocate, leaving behind our picturesque block and the girl waiting for us in the window. Then, I walked the dog two times daily from a friend's house in the city. We strolled by the chalk art walls, the pizza joint, the kebab shop, the quirky cafe that ironically resembled every other quirky cafe across the country, the dead rats (rest their souls), the dive bars, the fancy outdoor patios where I held my breath as we passed by, held it extra to offset the panting dog's deep, unknowing inhalations. For a time we didn't know if the dog could also get the contagion, for a time no one's breath could be trusted, not even his innocent stinking tongue could be tolerated.

But then it was fall and science said the virus didn't want the dog, only us; and by this time, I was walking him in our new town with a waterfall, while we continued to look for something more permanent. The dog took even further walks than before, with less traffic and dead rats to deter us. And the dog saw his first gorge, the dog saw his first black squirrel, the dog met his first backyard, never having had one before. And I must admit here, although it tragically disrupts my reliability as a narrator, that on the coldest days the dog did not walk, but was let out into this new, carved space to sniff, and doo, and trot along the fence line.

By the time we moved into our current home, the home we met the New Year in, fireworks let off outside our window as a delinquent greeting, the snow had fallen hard over the uneven sidewalks, and I had begun grumbling about having to walk the dog, my nose pink and raw, the bottoms of my feet white to match the season. But still we walked, the orange, gray glow of the winter sky at 4 p.m. as backdrop. The streetlights, a writer's fantasy, hazy beacons to help us reach the corner and back.

And when we returned, twice a day from the local tundra, we felt like we'd survived something, really survived something – and of course, we had. But how the dog shook off the cold as if it were nothing, ready to do it all again in the morning, clear sky or snowstorm. Sometimes I would shake off right next to him, an incantation of heat running through my once displaced, homed and re-homed body, and I realized that this, this is how you survive. The dog had known it best, had brought me through it all, had taught me this lesson (almost) twice daily: you just walk, and shake it off, and be ready to do it all again in the morning.

Acknowledgments

I would like to extend a special thanks to Steve Leard for his creative, thoughtful, patient work on the cover design for this book. I also owe a special debt to Hayley Higgs, a close friend and early supporter of this project who designed the logo for our website and branding. Steve and Hayley wrangled the sweeping concept behind this book into a memorable visual format.

When I started *Hindsight*, I never could have imagined the amount of work that would be required for this two-and-a-half-year endeavor; however, I can say with certainty that I never could have completed this book without the support of my family and friends. More specifically, I'm grateful to my mom and dad, who first encouraged me to pursue my passions and have never stopped supporting me; to my sister, Sam, whose discerning eye and impeccable judgment helped shape this book from its early stages into its final form; and to my wife, Haley, who endured the endless hours of deliberation and discussion, and who at every turn provided me with thoughtful, irreplicable feedback.

I'd also like to express my appreciation to anyone who submitted their story to Hindsight. I am no stranger to the victories and defeats of the publishing world, and I am truly humbled by the breadth and depth of stories we received during our call for submissions. Simply put, without the willingness of everyday people to share their stories, this book would never be in your hands.

About the Editor

Steve Fowler is a high school English teacher and former magazine editor, whose work has been featured in *Hudson Valley Magazine*, *The Valley Table*, *Northern Colorado Writers Anthology*, and *Social Media: The Academic Library Perspective*. He lives in the Hudson Valley region of New York State with his wife.

About the Writers

Julie Aitcheson is a freelance writer, author, and educator whose work has appeared in *Green Market Report*, *The Fresh Toast*, *Green Entrepreneur*, *Daily Press*, *LA Weekly*, *The Baltimore Sun*, and *The Chicago Tribune*, among other outlets. She received a full fellowship to the 2013 Stowe StoryLabs and won second place in the 2014 San Miguel Writers' Conference nonfiction writing competition. Her young adult novels include *Being Roy* (Finalist, 2017 Bisexual Book Awards) and *First Girl*, both from Harmony Ink Press.

Tanya Angell Allen is a freelance writer and library assistant at Yale University. She has published essays, reviews, and opinion editorials in such places as *The New York Times*, *The Hartford Courant*, and *New Pages*. She is currently researching the history and cultural significance of holidays.

Kendall Beck is currently in her freshman year at Taylor University in Indiana, pursuing studies in Multimedia Journalism and writing for the newspaper. She was born in the western suburbs of Chicago but recently moved to Nashville with her family, which has been a wonderful new adventure. When she's not writing professionally, or more often, furiously typing out lines of poetry in her Notes app, Kendall can be found at her local coffee shop, chasing the sunset with friends, or securing tickets to the next concert.

Michael Cannistraci began his creative journey as an actor. Having graduated from UCLA, he worked for thirty years acting in theater and television. In mid-life he answered a new calling and completed a Master's degree at Hunter College School of Social Work. He currently works as a clinical social worker and psychotherapist. His essays have been published in *Entropy Magazine*, *Literary Medical Messenger*, *The Evening Street Review*, *Bright Flash Literary Review*, *the Bangalore Review*, *The Dillydoun Review*, *East by Northeast*, *Stonecrop*, and *Iris Literary Review*.

Carlton Clayton lives in Charlotte, North Carolina and is a decorated, thirty-year Air Force veteran. He is a nonfiction writer who likes exploring adventure travel writing. He has completed essays chronicling his much-enjoyed treks up Mt. Kilimanjaro in Tanzania and Uluru in the Australian Outback, his journey along China's Great Wall, his descent into the belly of Giza's great pyramids, and navigating Norway's spectacular fiords. To that end, he's hoping that his pending adventure to Antarctica will be much more than journaling the takeoffs and landings of the albatross and the mating habits of penguins.

Storey Clayton recently received an MFA in creative nonfiction from West Virginia University. Currently a Grants Administrator at Drexel University's Dornsife School of Public Health, he's worked as a youth counselor, debate coach, strategic analyst, development director, rideshare driver, and poker player. His nonfiction has appeared in more than twenty literary journals, including *upstreet*, *Pleiades*, *Lunch Ticket*, *Typehouse Literary Magazine*, and *Blue Earth Review*. He lives in Philadelphia with his wife Alex and son Graham.

Joyeeta G. Dastidar, MD, is a hospitalist and clinical ethicist at New York Presbyterian-Columbia. She works to find ways to combine her interests in healthcare and the humanities, writing being one such bridge.

Ed Davis has immersed himself in writing and contemplative practices since retiring from college teaching. *Time of the Light*, a poetry collection, was released by Main Street Rag Press in 2013. His latest novel, *The Psalms of Israel Jones* (West Virginia University Press 2014), won the Hackney Award for an unpublished novel in 2010. Many of his stories, essays, and poems have appeared in anthologies and journals such as *Leaping Clear*, *Metafore*, *Hawaii Pacific Review*, and *Bacopa Literary Review*. He lives with his wife in the bucolic village of Yellow Springs, Ohio, where he bikes, hikes, meditates, and reads religiously.

Haitham Dinnawi is a visual creator with a strong base in human emotion and expressive storytelling. Photography came to him at a time when he needed it most. It fit his personality, his strengths. It had him constantly thinking, changing, growing, and it makes him feel alive to know that tomorrow will never be the same as today. He is inspired by light, music, travel, and vulnerability. He creates images that make viewers feel as if they are stepping into a dream. He is literally addicted to taking photographs, for which there is no known cure, except to make more!

Christine DiNovis Leonard is a high school English teacher in Lancaster County, Pennsylvania. She loves her profession, and greatly appreciates her colleagues and students. Her work has been featured in the *Nzuri Journal* and the *George Street Carnival*. Her children's novel, *Zebra Beeba*, was published in 2014 through Wee Creek Press. Christine enjoys attending musical theater productions with her four children and pondering new story ideas with her husband, Adam, who is also a fiction writer.

Roxanne Doty lives in Tempe, Arizona. Her first novel, *Out Stealing Water*, was published in August 2022 by *Regal House Publishing*. Her short story, ("Turbulence," *Ocotillo Review*) was nominated for the 2019 Pushcart Prize for short fiction. Other stories and poems have appeared in *Superstition Review*, *Forge*, *170 Review*, *Soundings Review*, *Four*

Chambers Literary Magazine, Lascaux Review, Lunaris Review, Journal of Microliterature, NewVerseNews, Saranac Review, Gateway Review, and *Reunion – The Dallas Review.*

Terri Elders, LCSW, a lifelong writer and editor, has been published in nearly 150 anthologies, including multiple editions of *Chicken Soup for the Soul.* She has written feature articles for countless national and international periodicals. Terri, a native Californian and a graduate of CSULB and UCLA, has lived and worked all over the world with the US Peace Corps. She is happy now to be back in Southern California, near family. She can be friended on Facebook and has an Amazon author page.

Duygu Eyrenci is a freelance copywriter and translator living in İzmir, Turkey. She has written two book and movie reviews for *Film Matters* magazine in 2013. Aside from professional and academic writing projects, she enjoys writing fiction, mainly sci-fi and fantasy, as a hobby. Her other interests include history, gender studies, traveling, and crafts.

Jose Francisco Fonseca is an Iraq war vet, warehouse worker, garbage guy, reader, and writer. He has lived in West Texas, and along the U.S. and Mexico border for thirty years.

Shelly Gill Murray is a freelance writer, a "My Life, My Story" writer in a trauma hospital, an ambassador for organ donation, a mission-based world traveler, a jail volunteer, and a former Ombudsman for crime victims. A story slam participant on *The Moth,* her essays can be found in *American Writers Review 2021, Gotham Writers,* the San Fedele Press eBook *Art in the Time of COVID-19, Mandala Magazine, Minnesota Women's Press, Pathways to Children.org, Caringbridge.org, Adoptive Families Magazine,* and *AAA Travel Magazine.* Ms. Gill Murray lives in Minneapolis with her husband and her old carrot-eating cockapoo.

Anne Gudger is an essay/memoir writer who writes hard and loves harder. She's been published in *Real Simple* Magazine, *The Rumpus*, *Tupelo Quarterly*, *PANK*, *Citron Review*, *Sweet Lit*, *Sunday Short Reads*, *CutBank*, *Cutthroat*, *Columbia Journal*, and elsewhere. Plus, she's won four essay contests and been a Best of the Net nominee twice. She's co-founder of Coffee and Grief, which includes a monthly reading series. Her debut memoir is forthcoming with Jaded Ibis Press in summer 2023. She lives in Banks, Oregon with her beloved husband.

Nathan Holic is the author of *Bright Lights, Medium-Sized City*, a not-so-medium-sized novel from Burrow Press. He is also the author of *The Things I Don't See* (a tiny but awesome novella, from Main Street Rag), and *American Fraternity Man* (a big big (yet equally awesome) novel, from Beating Windward Press), and is the Graphic Narrative Editor at *The Florida Review*.

Blair Hurley is the author of *The Devoted*, published by W.W. Norton, which was longlisted for The Center for Fiction's First Novel Prize. Her work is published or forthcoming in *Electric Literature*, *New England Review*, *The Georgia Review*, *Ninth Letter*, *Guernica*, *Paris Review Daily*, and elsewhere. She received a 2018 Pushcart Prize and two Pushcart Prize nominations in 2019.

Danielle Joffe writes personal essays, poems, and flash nonfiction. Her work can be found in *Hippocampus* and the *Waterwheel Review*. She is a nominee for a Pushcart Prize, Best of the Net, and a finalist for The Waking Flash Prose Prize. In her career as a spiritual psychologist and acupuncturist, she supports people through the unceasing transitions and transformations that life provides. She lives in the Berkshires of Western Massachusetts and is at work on her memoir.

Elizabeth Kleinfeld is an introvert and optimist who finds joy wherever it hides. She writes about being her husband's caregiver and widow and other uplifting topics at elizabethkleinfeld.com. Elizabeth is a faculty member at Metropolitan State University of Denver where she teaches courses on rhetoric and composition theory and practice. She lives in Denver with her two complicated dogs, travels every chance she gets, and eats dessert first.

Hannah Lund is a Chinese-English translator and writer currently based in Shanghai. She has a master's degree in comparative and world literature, and is the co-director of the Shanghai Writing Workshop's nonfiction group. Her work has appeared in *Speculative Nonfiction*, *MacQueen's Quinterly*, *Narrative*, *Sixth Tone*, *Atlas Obscura*, and *The Shanghai Literary Review*, among others.

Ebony Macfarlane lives in the Blue Mountains, west of Sydney in Australia. She is a primary school teacher by day, and an emerging writer by night. She spends much of her time exploring the beautiful area in which she is so fortunate to live, courageously battling deadly snakes and spiders. If she's not outside or spending time with her family, partner, and anthropomorphic dog, she is reading or writing. She most enjoys writing middle grade fiction for children.

Sumitra Mattai is a New York-based writer, textile designer, and mother of two. She holds a BFA in Textile Design from the Rhode Island School of Design and an MFA in Creative Writing from The New School. She explores themes of identity and culture in her work.

Heather C. Morris is a member of the Society for Children's Book Writers and Illustrators (SCBWI) and the 12x12 picture book challenge community. She coordinates a series on her website, "First Stories," to promote fellow writers by discussing the beginnings of their writing journeys, and her writing has been featured on multiple parenting websites, including Red Tricycle and Story Warren. But her greatest passion is her husband, three children, and three furry friends.

Kaitlyn Pacheco is a writer and editor living in Columbus, Ohio. She's previously written for publications like *Baltimore Magazine* and *Ohio Today*, and edited book products for brands like *Southern Living*, *Cooking Light*, and *Food & Wine*.

Ashlee Petrucci is an English teacher and writer living in Alberta, Canada. A wanderlust for travel has inspired worldwide explorations; one of which resulted in her first published story, "Marriage?" in the anthology *Emails from India: Women Write Home*. Another creative nonfiction story, "Love and Las Vegas," has also been published in *Chicken Soup for the Soul: Grandparents*. She is currently finishing her first novel.

Gabe Porter is a little man who writes words that he thinks are either funny or deep. Please agree with him so his worldview isn't shattered.

Paul Silvester is a father of two sons, a former primary school teacher of 30 years standing. He now leads guided tours at Winchester College, a reflection of the love he has for the history of the place where he lives. He enjoys cycling, running, and walking in the beautiful historic environment of Winchester. He loves trips to London to art galleries and theater, with and without friends. After working to instill a love of learning in his pupils, he now has more time for himself to keep learning, growing, and savoring the precious gift that is life.

Edwina Toulmin is a dentist living in Sydney who enjoys writing, cooking, and hanging out with her fur baby in her spare time.

Lenka Varekova is a nurse and a writer. She is originally from Czechoslovakia but after living and working in her favorite city for the last 20 years, she considers herself a New Yorker. She has always written stories in Czech, her native language, but now, after participating in the Writer's Guild Initiative workshop, she has started to write in English. Her piece was chosen and read by Meryl Streep at the Writer's Guild Initiative

Benefit Gala and by Alfre Woodard at the Workers Circle Benefit. She is currently working on a story based on her life under communism.

Nellie Warren is an eighteen-year-old Irish writer and artist. She has been writing since she was five years old and drawing since before she can remember. She has won awards at the International Fresh Film Festival and had two short stories published as a part of the Fighting Words supplement in the *Irish Times*.

Angelica Whitehorne is a writer from Buffalo, New York who has published or has forthcoming work in *Westwind Poetry*, *Mantis*, *The Laurel Review*, *The Cardiff Review*, *North Dakota Quarterly*, and *Air/Light Magazine*, among others. Besides being a devastated poet, Angelica is a Marketing Content Writer for a green energy loan company. She is also currently writing her first novel, so wish her luck!

Prompts for Discussion

Use the following questions as a springboard for conversation in book groups, classrooms, or over a cup of coffee.

1. Which story in the collection did you relate to the most? What elements of the story did you connect with?

2. How did the portrayal of the initial COVID-19 outbreak compare with your memory of events?

3. What was your favorite line from the book? Explain why this line stood out to you in particular.

4. What similarities do these stories share? How do they tie together?

5. How do you think the organization of the book reflected the experience of living through 2020? Was there anything you would change about the way the book is structured?

6. If you could ask the editor of this book one question, what would it be?

7. What do you think of the book's title? How does it relate to the book's contents? What other title might you choose?

8. What do you think the editor's purpose was in publishing this book? What ideas was he trying to get across?

9. What questions do you still have after reading this book?

10. Do you think any of the stories in this anthology could be expanded into a full-length book?

Editor's Request

Hindsight was made possible through the hard work and dedication of myself and a small group of contributors, freelance designers, family, and friends. There are no publishing companies – large or small – involved in the production, publication, or promotion of *Hindsight*, which is to say that this book relies more than most on word of mouth and personal recommendations. As such, if you enjoyed this collection, I ask that you take 5 minutes and leave a review. You can find the link to do so on our website at www.hindsightbook2020.com.

Similarly, if you know of someone who would appreciate this anthology or identify with one of the stories in it, please let them know. The ultimate purpose of *Hindsight* is not only to connect us with our human side, but to connect us with each other as well.

Thank you for taking the time to read this book. I hope your experience reading it was as worthwhile as mine was editing it.

Sincerely,

Steve Fowler

Made in the USA
Middletown, DE
30 March 2023

27239441R00121